Ast

WHY ARE YOU IN MY LIFE?

Also by Beverly Flynn

Astrology & Weight Control: The Jupiter/Pluto Connection

Astrology & Money: What's Your Wealth Quotient?

Astrology & Difficult Relationships:

WHY ARE YOU IN MY LIFE?

Beverly Flynn

TLH PUBLISHING COMPANY

Copyright © 2006
Beverly Flynn

All rights reserved. No part of this book may be reproduced in any form, except for the inclusion of brief quotations in a review, without permission in writing from the author or publisher.

LCCN 2006901942
ISBN: 978-0-9758583-2-5

First Printing   February 2006

TLH PUBLISHING COMPANY
1845 Cambria Avenue
Landers, CA 92285

Printed in the United States by Morris Publishing
3212 East Highway 30
Kearney, NE 68847
1-800-650-7888

To my sons, Christopher and Matthew, the great joys of my life, and to my mother who started it all.

TABLE OF CONTENTS

Introduction		9
CH 1	Astrology & Relating	13
CH 2	Astrology Basics	21
CH 3	Categorizing Difficult Relationships	40
CH 4	If the Relationship is Unbearable	60
CH 5	Obstacles to Relating	73
CH 6	Will the Relationship Improve?	81
CH 7	Walking in Another's Shoes	100
CH 8	When Should We Take Action?	132
CH 9	How to Analyze your Difficult Relationships	136
CH 10	There is No Such Thing as a Difficult Relationship	146
Sources		173

INTRODUCTION

I once overheard a young woman at a restaurant telling her friend that she dreaded the holidays because she always had to spend them with her parents. She said that she was considering skipping the visit this Christmas because she had absolutely nothing in common with her parents, and that when they were together, all they ever did was fight. Her parents didn't approve of her lifestyle and they didn't like her friends. Basically everything she did was wrong in their eyes. She couldn't figure out why the universe had chosen to give her this particular set of parents.

The young woman's words stayed with me, and I thought about her and her situation for a long time. Her story touched me not because it was so unusual, because it was not. In fact, many of us find ourselves in uncomfortable relationships with those close to us. Just like her, we can't figure out why we are in them, or how the relationship progressed to such a low point. Her story stayed with me, though, because of the frustration and hopelessness in her voice. She was totally at a loss as to how to proceed, and that is what I want to address in this book. Many of us, when we reach that level of frustration and hopelessness in a close relationship, choose to simply give up on it, when in fact we may be walking away from important life lessons, experiences, support and love. In addition, giving up on close relationships sets us up for a lifetime of guilt and regret, and begins the pattern of running away rather than facing a difficult situation.

The young woman in the restaurant needed help in making sense of her relationship with her parents, and she also needed advice on how to improve the problem areas. So it was in the process of pondering her situation that I decided to write this book, and hence the title, *"Why Are You In My Life?"* with the hope that it will aid others who are struggling just as she was with relationship issues.

In the case of parents, children, siblings, and other close blood relatives, we are often forced to deal with very frustrating situations, and this is made even more unbearable because of the fact that these are people that we cannot avoid. If we were in a bad marriage, we would have the option of divorce open to us. With relatives, though, this option does not exist. We can, of course, decide to cut off all contact with troublesome relatives, but the issues will still remain and can haunt us for the remainder of our lives, causing tremendous psychological and emotional problems. We may think that we have abandoned a relationship, and physically maybe we have, but subconsciously the relationship still lives on. A better solution in dealing with stressful close relationships is to figure out the real cause of the problem and work on eliminating it.

Difficult relationships are those relationships with people who are in our lives every day that we simply cannot run away from even though we may want to. These kinds of difficult relationships often include others who are not necessarily blood relatives. In-laws, for instance, can be the cause of difficult relationship issues. Or, you may be fighting with your son's elementary school principal or be frustrated with a specific teacher. Your boss, a co-worker, or the man who lives next door can also create those kinds of uncontrollable and uninvited tense relationships that need to be addressed and healed. These can all be classified as difficult relationships because they involve people that we are forced to deal with.

For want of a better term, I have chosen to use the word "difficult" to describe these tense, stressful, and frustrating relationships. The word "difficult" implies that even though there

INTRODUCTION

are problems, there is the hope of a solution, as opposed to other words I could have chosen, such as "impossible," which implies no possibility of improvement, or "hopeless," implying no chance of a cure. Difficult relationships are messy; they do make our blood pressure rise, and they can cause us to say and do things that we normally wouldn't say or do. Difficult relationships can make us hurt inside, and sometimes because of the hurt, we do things that later make us ashamed of our actions. Difficult relationships generate anger and frustration. They can make us feel as if we have no control over the situation. And yet, many, if not all, of the causes of the pain and anger and frustration can be addressed, and so most stressful relationships are not hopeless or impossible; they are only difficult.

Unless you live in a vacuum, all of us have, at one time, had to deal with a difficult relationship. That is the nature of being a human being who has to interact with other human beings. Perhaps you are estranged from your children, and can't figure out what to do to heal the relationship and end the separation. Or maybe you have a particular friend or neighbor whose sole mission is to sabotage your life. Sometimes difficult relationships manifest as power struggles with your boss or some other authority figure, or with a co-worker. Difficult relationships abound, and we are almost always at a loss as to how to handle them. Our normal reaction is usually either to fight and create an even bigger rift, or to painfully acquiesce to the desires and wishes of the other person, all the while seething on the inside. The final resort is usually a total abandonment of the relationship.

This book focuses on those relationships that are ostensibly out of our control, those relationships that seem to have a life and quality of their own, separate from the two people involved, those difficult relationships that we cannot escape from and yet are powerless to do anything about. In this book, we will investigate the astrological reasons behind that feeling of powerlessness, and also look at the nature of the relationship

Astrology & Difficult Relationships: WHY ARE YOU IN MY LIFE?

itself, analyzing it to determine its true significance. Once we can categorize the relationship, that is, give it a name, we can then begin to understand why it exists in its current state, and more importantly, we can determine those things that we need to do in order to change it from a difficult relationship into an enjoyable one. The normal ways of dealing with difficult relationships i.e., arguing and fighting, suffering in silence, or giving up on it entirely, are all extremely negative ways of handling problems. Something in the middle is more appropriate, a solution that benefits both parties involved, and that will force the relationship to grow in the right direction. The purpose of this book is to help you find the middle ground, to identify the appropriate actions for improving the relationship so that the pain ends and true enjoyment can begin. And we will go one step further in this book. We will teach you skills based on your astrology that will enable you to arrive at the point where you will see that there is no such thing as a difficult relationship.

Some of the things that you will have to do may be painful at first, but isn't it better to endure a little pain that results from change than to suffer in an unbearable relationship for the rest of your life? And sometimes the steps required to fix a relationship are not painful at all; you may discover that you already possess the necessary tools and have just never considered using them. But before you can fix your difficult relationships, you must be able to identify them for what they are, that is, you must be able to answer that most basic of questions, *why are you in my life?*

CHAPTER 1

ASTROLOGY & RELATING

"The meeting of two personalities is like the contact of two chemical substances: if there is any reaction, both are transformed." Carl Jung

Astrology is a science that allows us to better understand the workings of the universe. It is a manual or handbook for deciphering cosmic laws. It is a map of the relationships between the planets, signs, and houses. It is an indicator of the precise and economic use of energy and force by the universe. Therefore, it can be said that astrology is proof that nothing in the universe happens by accident. There is a reason or purpose for everything and everything follows universal law. There is indeed a master plan. It is through the study of astrology and the inter-relationships of the planets, signs and houses that we are able to better understand these universal laws that preside over the unfolding of the master plan of the cosmos.

If we accept the premise that everything that happens in the universe is according to universal law, then we should be able to apply those same universal laws to our personal relationships as well, since our own little universe is a microcosm of the greater cosmos. In other words, when difficult or troublesome people

Astrology & Difficult Relationships: WHY ARE YOU IN MY LIFE?

appear in our lives, they are there for a reason. They are part of the unfolding master plan of our life.

The universe seeks balance, and so a person, a smaller version of the macrocosm that is the universe, must also seek balance. Astrologers often refer to this constant striving towards balance as karma. Karma is a universal law, and could be defined as the force generated by a person's actions. So, karma is really just the law of balance. We define karma in many ways in our culture, but the meaning is the same. We say things such as, "You reap what you sow," or, "What goes around comes around," etc. Many people like to refer to karma as good or bad, but really it is neither. It is simply the law of cause and effect. It is the result of your actions. Newton's way of describing this karmic law or effect was "For every action, there is an equal and opposite reaction."

Karma doesn't necessarily imply a past life connection, although it can. A karmic relationship simply means that there is a balancing that needs to occur or a lesson that needs to be learned by one or both of the parties, and the universe has determined that this particular relational interaction is the most effective way to either accomplish this balancing and/or to teach the needed lesson. Many of us wince when we hear the word "karma" because we automatically associate it with trouble or difficulty and so the thought of a karmic relationship is assumed to be troubling or difficult. But while troubling relationships can usually be classified as karmic, they really are not as negative as a lot of people would make them out to be. The real reason that some relationships are harder to handle than others is because there is a lesson somewhere to be learned and we are having trouble learning it. If we subscribe to the view that life is a school, then we should want to learn as much as we can while we are in it. If all relationships were easy, there would be no soul growth. Therefore, we should relish these karmic and challenging relationships as opportunities to grow and achieve balance.

ASTROLOGY & RELATING

Whenever two people interact, both parties will be affected, even if it doesn't appear that way on the surface. If the relationship is functioning properly, both persons benefit in some way. For instance, if we have done something at some point in time to harm another person, than an equal and opposite action will be required in order to keep things in balance in the relationship. The person who injured or harmed the other party benefits from this balancing action because he is learning to replace inappropriate behavior with something that is appropriate, and he is being given a chance to make amends. The person who was previously harmed benefits by receiving a payment, so to speak, for the harm done to them in the past, again balancing things out.

Karmic relationships do not always have to do with repayment of debts. Karmic parings exist in many forms and for many reasons. You could, for instance, be in a relationship because the two of you have similar areas of your lives that are out of balance, and you want to work together on the same issue in this lifetime. In other words, you want to help each other along. For example, you may have a tendency to be overly emotional and have a very close friend who also has this tendency, only more so. When the two of you are together, you act as a tranquilizer for her emotional outbursts, which is your gift to her, and at the same time, you are reminded of what you could become if you allowed your emotions to progress in that direction, her gift to you. So through this karmic relationship, both of you benefit.

Karmic ties, then, exist between people for imparting life lessons and for balancing an unbalanced life. They are not mean or heavy-handed punishments for evil actions we did in the past, which is how karma is often explained in metaphysical books. Everything in the universe is done from a point of love, and so the lessons that we are being asked to learn via our relationships are for our own well-being and spiritual growth. Karmic relationships help us to identify the areas where we have made incorrect choices in the past, and areas where we need to learn more appropriate behaviors.

Astrology & Difficult Relationships: WHY ARE YOU IN MY LIFE?

If we looked at all difficult relationships as learning and balancing opportunities lovingly given to us by the universe, then our lives would be much happier and our relationships would improve.

One of the reasons that we dislike karmic or difficult relationships so much is that they can tend to make us feel powerless, when in fact we are not. The opposite is actually more correct. The reason we feel powerless is that we are choosing to react to the relationship in the wrong way, and therefore are continuing to make incorrect choices. Each time we make the wrong choices, things don't go the way we want them to go, and so we feel powerless.

Symptoms of feeling powerless in a relationship include avoidance, excuse making, feigned or real illness, and carried to the extreme, total severance of the relationship. At the other end of the spectrum is total capitulation to the wishes of the other individual, ignoring your feelings and point of view altogether. None of these responses are appropriate and some of them are quite detrimental to our mental, physical and emotional health and/or possibly to the mental, physical and emotional health of the other person as well.

The proper solution for dealing with difficult relationships is to figure out the reason for the relationship, which will then allow you to figure out the correct way to react to and deal with the relationship, and then the feeling of powerlessness will vanish. Once we know the nature and purpose of a relationship, we will no longer feel out of control, and we will know what to do to turn the relationship around. Once we turn the relationship around, frustration and anger will be replaced with peace and contentment, for we will be secure in the knowledge that the relationship is progressing in the way that it should for the right reasons.

The way that we discover the true nature of the relationship is through the science of astrology. Astrology can help us reach that point of peace and contentment by helping us to understand the laws of the universe as they apply to our lives.

ASTROLOGY & RELATING

When we understand the rules, when we know what is expected of us and why, we can then make appropriate decisions and choices.

Astrology allows us to look analytically and unemotionally at the energies involved in the union, thus clearly delineating the type of relationship, the reason for it, and the hoped for result. Additionally, astrology will give clues as to the appropriate handling of the situation, and will point out the tools available to both parties to carry out the appropriate plan.

Of course, all of this astrological analysis can be accomplished easily by comparing the two charts of the individuals involved. But if the chart of one of the involved individuals is not known, then the analysis becomes a little more difficult. Not impossible, but more difficult. If only one chart is available, then some intuitional interpolating will be necessary to come up with a diagnosis and to formulate a plan of action. We will discuss ways of dealing with partnerships where only one chart is available later on in the book. For now, you only need to understand that the process involves looking at the relationship from the perspective of both of the parties involved in order to correctly determine its nature and the appropriate response. Your required response may be quite different from that of the other person in the partnership, but you are only responsible for your response. It is up to the other person to do his or her part.

Suppose the other person refuses to do his or her part, you are thinking. Won't that sabotage your efforts? The answer is that in many cases the other person will be reluctant at first to change, but this should not discourage you. If you act appropriately, your actions can sometimes cause a change in the other person. The source of the friction between the two of you was more than likely an inappropriate reaction to the nature of the relationship, so if one of you changes his behavior in the partnership, there is a very strong likelihood that the other person will act in kind. Of course it is always better if both persons are consciously committed to doing the necessary work to mend the

Astrology & Difficult Relationships: WHY ARE YOU IN MY LIFE?

relationship, but if only one is consciously working on the relationship, progress can still be made. For instance, suppose that your conversations with your roommate almost always end up in a shouting match. You decide that you want to make a change in the relationship to eliminate all of the yelling and shouting. You bring up a contentious subject, and sure enough, your roommate begins yelling. You, though, refuse to lose your temper this time. You speak clearly and rationally, but remain calm. Gradually, your roommate realizes that she is the only one shouting, and she begins to calm down and speak quietly also, thus allowing the two of you to pass a communication hurdle in your relationship together even though you were the person who initiated the action.

Sometimes you may find that the other person has no interest in trying to fix the relationship, and that the only efforts toward improvement are coming from you. An estranged relative, for instance, may be quite content not having to communicate with you, and may be staunchly against your initial efforts at making contact, however innocent they may be. If you are the only one interested in fixing the relationship, suggestions will be given later on as to how to draw out a reluctant friend or relative, and you may have to settle for very little and very slow progress, at least initially. Again, a careful assessment of the astrological indicators of the relationship will assist in determining the degree of progress to be expected.

Now that we know that there is hope to fix troubled relationships, we need to make sure that we have correctly identified the troubled or difficult relationships in our life so that we can begin to work on them. Most of us come into contact with people every day, and yet in most cases, none of them would be classified as difficult. Usually, though, if we are asked about a relationship and our first reaction is to point out what is wrong with the other person, then more than likely it is a relationship that needs some help. The thing that separates difficult relationships from other relationships is the amount of negative energy we devote to them. The energy can be mental, emotional or physical. Worrying, arguing, accusing, debating, yelling, lying, etc., are the prime indicators that something is wrong in the relationship. If you spend large amounts of your time lamenting something you did to that particular person or vice versa, if you cry often because of the relationship, if the relationship is constantly on your mind, or if you replay conversations with that person over and over in your head, then more than likely, this is a troubled relationship.

If you are in denial, that is, if you are dealing with a difficult relationship and are not labeling it as such, you are slowing down the process and delaying your chances of fixing the relationship. Admitting that there is a problem is sometimes a major step, but it has to be done before any changes can be made. Let me give you an example. Suppose you have a daughter-in-law that you feel is absolutely the rudest person you have ever met. You don't say anything to her or your son because you don't want to be labeled as a meddling or mean mother-in-law. So you keep your feelings to yourself, and smile whenever you are around her. You see that she is starting to pass on her negative traits to your grandchildren, but you don't want to say anything for fear of affecting your relationship with your grandchildren. By not addressing the issue of rudeness in a timely manner, you have allowed a negative trait to be passed on to others.

If you are on the other end, in other words, you are the one causing problems for the other person, this can manifest in two ways. The first way is that you are totally unaware that the other person considers you to be difficult. The second is that you are aware, and either don't care or don't wish to do anything to change the dynamics of the relationship because you are satisfied. If you are the first person, the one who is unaware that you are being perceived as being difficult, then after reading this book, you may begin to gain some insights into all of your relationships, and hopefully, they will all improve. If you are the second person,

Astrology & Difficult Relationships: WHY ARE YOU IN MY LIFE?

after reading this book, you may wish to change your attitude about your relationships because hopefully you will see the benefits to be gained when both of you alter your behavior.

    The bottom line is that astrology does provide hope for resolving difficult relationships. Knowing is half the battle, and if you know why someone is in your life, then you are well on your way to making the most of the relationship. Astrology can allow you to truly answer the question, "Why are you in my life?" through an intelligent and scientific investigation of the factors forming the relationship. Then, using your intuition, you can take all of this knowledge and turn it into a clear and concise understanding of the nature of the relationship. From there, again with the help of astrology, you should be able to intuit the proper behavior required to put the relationship on the right path. Relating to others should be a beautiful, harmonious and enjoyable activity. So if something is blocking your ability to have beautiful, harmonious relationships, then we want to find out what it is and fix it as quickly as possible.

CHAPTER 2

ASTROLOGY BASICS

Since astrology is a science, there are certain basic terms and concepts that must be mastered before we can begin working with it. The angles, signs, planets and houses all have different meanings and significances which must be understood, and because we are dealing with relationships in this book, these generic definitions must be modified to include the relationship between two astrological charts. The signs and planets are transmitters of energies (the signs relating more to higher level or soul consciousness, and the planets relating more to personality integration), and the houses represent the areas of life where the energies are active. Universal laws regulate the effects caused by the interplay of the energies of the signs, planets, and houses, and so a basic understanding of their meaning is essential.

Starting with the angles, we will look at the meanings from a strictly relationship perspective. Next, we will define the meanings of the signs, the planets, the most commonly used asteroids, and the major aspects in relationship astrology. The definitions that are being presented in this chapter include the traditional astrological meanings and so will be a review for many of you. In later chapters, we will be expanding or enlarging upon some of these definitions, but for now, they will give us the needed base and a similar starting point in our examination of relationships, and will enable us to begin the process of categorizing relationships in Chapter Three.

THE ANGLES

ASCENDANT

The Ascendant is the sign on the cusp of the first house. Technically, it is the point where the horizon intersects the ecliptic. In a relationship, the aspects made to the Ascendant of either party are extremely important. The Ascendant represents the higher nature or soul purpose, or the person we are striving to be, so how another person's planets relate to our higher self can be extremely beneficial for the relationship as a whole if the aspects are positive. If they are difficult aspects, conflicts can occur because the higher self of either party has to be able to express itself fully in order for the relationship to function at its optimal level. Difficult aspects to the Ascendant of either party usually require that the relationship be taken to a higher, more spiritual level if progress is to be made.

DESCENDANT

The Descendant is the sign on the cusp of the seventh house, and is always opposite the Ascendant. The Descendant represents those traits that are opposite our own, or the traits that are hidden or lacking in our nature. Therefore, in a relationship, the traits of the Descendant can be indicative of the traits we look for in a mate or partner, and thus the saying opposites attract. If the Descendant of one person is positively related to planets in another person's chart, then the two people should together be able to form a well-rounded relationship. If not, the differences will identify weakness and holes, hindering the growth of the relationship until they are resolved.

NADIR

The Nadir is the sign on the cusp of the fourth house and represents the bottom of a chart, the foundation or the roots. So if the Nadir is highlighted in a relationship, something involving the basic beliefs or foundational values of the parties is being highlighted. The relationship may be looking to change these values, or to shore them up and make them stronger. Or, the relationship may simply reflect that the two parties have similar values or roots, and that they can therefore use this common base as a springboard to other activities.

MIDHEAVEN

The Midheaven is the sign on the cusp of the tenth house. It is always opposite the Nadir. The tenth house represents one's career, profession or standing in the world. One's career or calling is quite important and people whose charts make aspects to our Midheaven will influence our career and public standing in one way or another, either positively or negatively. When someone has positive aspects to our Midheaven, they can be instrumental in our worldly success, and if they negatively aspect our Midheaven, then they can have the opposite effect, either slowing or totally blocking our worldly progress.

VERTEX

The vertex is similar to an angle. It is the point where the prime vertical intercepts the ecliptic. It is usually interpreted as

Astrology & Difficult Relationships: WHY ARE YOU IN MY LIFE?

a point of destiny or fate, meaning that it represents something that must be done in our lifetime, and it usually has to do with personal relationships. Obviously, the Vertex is quite important in relationship astrology, then, because it indicates that something about the relationship is fated or karmic. And while a fated or karmic relationship does not necessarily imply a difficult relationship, it does indicate that there is some aspect of the relationship that must be resolved. It is a relationship that cannot be avoided, and thus the destined or karmic aspect.

ANTI-VERTEX

The Anti-vertex is the point opposite the Vertex, and so is interpreted as the point of freedom. It is the freedom we have earned because we have met and properly handled our fate or destiny, and so are now liberated. A relationship involving the Anti-vertex of either person is one that should give both parties a lot of freedom and a sense of empowerment to take the relationship in whatever direction they wish to take it.

SIGNS

ARIES

Aries is the first sign of the zodiac, and represents initiative, new beginnings, a pioneering spirit, and entrepreneurship. Relationships emphasizing the sign of Aries are going to be new and fresh, and the parties won't be afraid to test new ways of relating. Negatively, this type of relationship could mean that the Aries person may appear to be aggressive, rude or brash to the other party, for Aries always wants to rush forward and try the new and unexplored, sometimes without thinking things through, or without always following established rules and traditions.

TAURUS

In relationships, if Taurus is highlighted, the parties are going to seek more traditional ways of relating, and they are going to very reluctant to change or try new things. Taurus will, however, bring in a large dose of stability and reliability that every relationship needs to be successful. On a higher level, the Taurean gift of vision can be used to help them see the higher possibilities and spiritual purpose of the relationship.

GEMINI

Gemini energy will allow the participants in the relationship to see both sides of the issue, a trait that is very conductive to proper relating. Being able to see both sides allows for better communication, and the fact that the energy is air or mental ensures that the relating will not be colored by personal desires and emotions. Rational and thoughtful discussions, with comments, and ideas contributed by both parties should be the result.

CANCER

Cancer is the mother and nurturer, giving birth and then nurturing their creations. As the nurturing sign of the zodiac, Cancerian energy gives the relationship the sensitivity to understand each other's feelings, allowing them to intuitively know what needs to be done to correct any problems. The parties in the relationship will nurture and take care of each other. Negatively, Cancer can be an energy that likes to hold onto the past, and this tendency has to be overcome for the relationship to progress.

LEO

The sign of Leo brings with it the highly recognized strong

Astrology & Difficult Relationships: WHYA RE YOU IN MY LIFE?

sense of self-identity, and if the energy is being utilized in the highest way, the relationship will exude magnanimity and big-heartedness. A kind and dignified approach to relating can be the result. Also, because Leos like to have fun, there may be a real sense of joy and pleasure in the relationship. Negatively, if the Leo person exhibits the lower, self-centered aspect of Leo, the result can be an unbalanced relationship, with the Leo person controlling the other person or wielding power incorrectly.

VIRGO

The sign of Virgo brings with it the idea of purity, discrimination, and perfection. Thus, relationships where Virgo is involved would be striving towards faultless relating. When the relationship is functioning properly, this can create a very refined and detail-oriented combination, and a shared dedication to service. Carried to extremes, though, this striving for perfection can also create a lot of criticism and bickering between the parties, obviously a detriment to healthy relating.

LIBRA

When Libra is involved in a relationship, much emphasis is placed on making the right decisions regarding the relationship, and basically relating to each other in the correct and fair way. Libra wants everything in balance, and when the partnership follows the karmic laws of relating, including respect for the other person, treating the other person the way you would like to be treated, and fulfilling your responsibilities to the partnership, then the desired balance will be achieved, and the relationship will be able to function at its highest.

SCORPIO

Scorpio energy usually brings with it some kind of testing or crisis situations, so a scorpionic relationship will be full of crises and struggles, and it may not be the easiest of relationships to deal with. The lessons to be learned, though, will be valuable and worth the extra effort. Whenever we reach a point of crisis in a relationship, we must make a decision about which way we are going to go in the relationship, and assuming that during these periods of struggle, we make the correct decision, we help the relationship grow in strength and power.

SAGITTARIUS

Sagittarius represents single-mindedness, that is, the person who is either on a mission, or who is so sure of his moral, philosophical and/or spiritual views that he is able to be a guide for others. In relationships, then, Sagittarius brings with it a sense of direction, a sense of moral values or a moral or spiritual code. A relationship where Sagittarius is highlighted will be one that can set a moral example for others if the underlying motives are correct.

CAPRICORN

Capricorn is the sign that represents the highest that one can achieve, so in relationships, this energy will bring a strong commitment to the goals of the relationship and a striving to succeed. A political partnership, for instance, would likely have Capricorn very strongly placed, as would a business partnership formed to succeed in the financial world. At a higher level, Capricorn can bring to a partnership the ability to achieve very lofty spiritual goals, the mountaintop experience.

Astrology & Difficult Relationships: WHY ARE YOU IN MY LIFE?

AQUARIUS

This is the sign of the humanitarian, and so in relationships where Aquarius is involved, the potential exists for developing a true sense of sharing and understanding; the two persons involved in the relationship have no problem in making decisions based upon the good of the partnership rather than the individual. At its highest level, this partnership will demonstrate a sense of equality and support for each other's right to think and say and feel what they truly believe, and a uniting in service to others.

PISCES

Pisces is the sign of true compassion and love. Thus, in a relationship where Pisces is prominent, the people are able to look for and find the best in each other. The relationship also has a compassionate, understanding and empathetic nature. On the negative side, they must avoid becoming too emotional in their relationship, the lower level of compassion, lest the compassion and understanding degenerate into self-pity and lack of direction.

THE PLANETS

SUN

The Sun traditionally represents the personal or lower self, and all matters of personal self-expression. In a relationship where the Sun of either party is involved, the self-expression or creativity of that party is somehow being limited or tested, or positively, spurred on to higher heights, depending of the nature of the aspects involved. Since the Sun highlights, some area of the other person's life is being highlighted or focused upon.

MOON

The Moon represents the past, and all ingrained emotional and habitual responses. It also relates to your foundation and your early home life. In a relationship, it can often indicate a past karmic tie, or an area of life that needs to be eliminated or at least updated and/or brought under control.

MERCURY

Mercury has most to do with communication, intelligence, and thought processes, although it can also relate to the more spiritual issue of connecting the higher and lower self. In a relationship, then, Mercury's involvement can be indicative of the level of communication in the relationship, and on a higher level, it can indicate that one person is in some way helping or impeding the progress of the other person in contacting their higher self.

VENUS

Venus is the planet of love, beauty, and harmony. On one level, this can represent passionate love, for instance romantic love between a man and a woman. The higher level love that Venus represents is that of unconditional, intelligent and impersonal love. So if Venus is involved in a relationship, some aspect of showing or giving love is being highlighted, and depending upon the level of spiritual development of the parties involved, so will be the level of the love being addressed.

MARS

Mars has to do with personal desires and passions, vitality, energy and aggression. In a relationship, the Martian person is bringing the energy and passion that can fire up the relationship.

Astrology & Difficult Relationships: WHY ARE YOU IN MY LIFE?

If used positively, this energy can help the relationship to accomplish many things; if used negatively, it can cause the relationship to become highly competitive, argumentative, and possibly aggressive.

JUPITER

Jupiter brings joy, happiness and optimism in general, so whenever Jupiter is involved in a relationship it is very fortunate, for Jupiter will expand the kind feelings that the two parties have for each other. There is a spiritual element related to Jupiter and so the relationship will be blessed in a way. Even in hard aspect, a relationship touched by Jupiter will have a warmth and joy about it that will be easy to discern, and the two people involved will be ready and willing to expand their relationship. They just need to learn a little temperance and wise judgment.

SATURN

Saturn is related to karma and karmic rewards and punishments, so if Saturn is involved in a relationship, there is definitely a serious feel to it. The sense of duty, loyalty or responsibility will be strong, for Saturn, as the disciplinarian of the zodiac, sees to it that we meet our relationship responsibilities. In relationships where commitment is important, e.g. marriages or business partnerships, Saturn's involvement should be welcomed. Whenever one or other of the parties does not want to live up to their responsibilities to the relationship, then the feeling of being imprisoned or restricted will be the result.

URANUS

Always expect the unexpected with Uranus. Uranus shakes up relationships in an attempt to get rid of any outmoded behaviors or patterns and replace them with more appropriate ones. Whether or not the energy of Uranus is welcomed in the relationship depends upon the level of spiritual development of the individuals involved; those more highly evolved will be able to see the changes Uranus brings to the relationship as being changes for the better; those not so highly evolved are likely to fight against the changes and see them as disruptive.

NEPTUNE

Neptune, at its highest level, brings idealism into all of our relationships, thus allowing us to clearly visualize the best that the relationship could be. However, on a lower level, or if the energy is responded to in a negative way, it can blind us and/or cause us to be deceived by our own defective interpretations of the situation. It can also lead to denial of truth, and to all manner of addictive and escapist behavior. Whether the higher or lower aspect of Neptune will function in a relationship is based upon the aspects made to it, and upon the level of development of the parties involved.

PLUTO

Pluto acts as a transformer in relationships, bringing deeply hidden issues to the surface so that they can be dealt with and removed or redeemed. The purpose of Pluto is to rid us of anything standing in the way of true spiritual progress in the relationship. Therefore, we don't always understand the reasons why things happen in relationships where Pluto is prominent; Pluto keeps us in the dark sometimes. These relationships can sometimes have a very sinister feel, again related to the fact that Pluto rules the underworld, that which is hidden or below the surface.

Astrology & Difficult Relationships: WHY ARE YOU IN MY LIFE?

ASTEROIDS

CHIRON

Chiron represents areas where we are wounded and can be subsequently healed, so in a relationship, this is an indication that the relationship itself can be wounding to or healing for one or both of the parties. In mythology, Chiron was also a very wise teacher, embracing the idea of learning through pain, and thus healing ourselves. Chiron in mythology was also a centaur, and so is related to horses and the sign Sagittarius in that it has a clear vision or sense of the direction the partnership should take.

JUNO

Juno represents the committed partner, usually a marriage partner, but can also be a business partner, or anyone with whom we are in a relationship that requires a close personal commitment. Therefore, this is a very fortunate asteroid to have in a relationship requiring commitment because it is an indication that at least one of the partners takes the relationship seriously and is dedicated to its survival.

CERES

Ceres is similar in effect to the Moon and the sign Cancer, in that it is related to nurturing of the other person. Ceres in mythology presided over the harvests, so the asteroid is also related to bringing something to fruition, as in the harvest of an idea, event, project, etc. In a relationship, the Ceres person would be the nurturer and the relationship itself would show great promise of bringing something to fruition.

VESTA

Vesta relates to whatever we are totally dedicated to, so in a relationship, Vesta would indicate a partnership or union dedicated to a cause, a person or to the relationship itself. The meaning of this energy carries more of a sense of duty and sacrifice with it, as the archetypes were the Vestal Virgins in mythology who guarded the sacred flame and who were sworn to chastity.

PALLAS ATHENE

In mythology, Pallas Athene sprang from the head of Jupiter, thus this asteroid is associated with intelligence and strategic ability. A partnership with Pallas Athene prominent would be very good at winning battles of any sort, because of the combined mental prowess of the parties, and the unparalled strategic ability available to the partnership.

HOUSES

FIRST HOUSE

The first house deals with you, that is, how you look, how others perceive you, and how you perceive the world. It is about your self-expression, the ease or difficulty in being yourself and in having others understand and relate to that self. From a spiritual perspective, it has to do with the expression or emergence of your higher level, or soul purpose. In relationships, the way you express yourself can be aided or blocked based upon the dynamics of the relationship.

Astrology & Difficult Relationships: WHY ARE YOU IN MY LIFE?

SECOND HOUSE

The second house deals with personal resources, your ability to earn a living, and your possessions. But more importantly, the second house deals with values, your personal values and your personal worth, and on a higher level, your spiritual resources and values. In relationships, the idea of joint values becomes important. What you feel is important or "worth"-while is emphasized in a partnership. Additionally, a second house emphasis in a relationship can be an indication of the treasures that are possessed by that partnership that can be used to fulfill some joint purpose, and these treasures may be material or otherwise.

THIRD HOUSE

The third house has deals with immediate surroundings, education, and communication, and on a spiritual level, it has to do with relating the higher and lower selves, or the soul and personality. When the third house is involved in a relationship, then communications between the parties will be affected positively or negatively, based on the planets in the third house and the aspects made to them. Positive aspects would indicate that communication in the relationship should be good, and negative aspects obviously indicate that communication problems need to be resolved.

FOURTH HOUSE

The fourth house relates to our base or foundation, emotional, psychological, and on a spiritual level, the foundation or anchoring of the higher self or soul. In personal relationships, it is an indication of the underlying issues holding the relationship together. Ideas and ideals are firmly rooted in the fourth house, and so whatever is firmly rooted in the relationship will show up and so whatever is firmly rooted in the relationship will show up here. It is also an indication of the emotional nature of the relationship, that is, how the two people respond emotionally to issues with which they are confronted.

FIFTH HOUSE

The fifth house deals with creativity and our special talents or gifts, and the expression, on a higher level, of our special soul talents. So the special gifts or talents of the relationship are to be found here. What the two of you can do together that you could not do alone will be highlighted. Issues relating to children will also show up here. Also, since the fifth house has to do with fun and romance and social activities, the opportunity exists for this to be a very enjoyable and creative joint venture.

SIXTH HOUSE

The sixth house deals with work, routine activities, service to others and health issues. Especially at the soul level, the sixth house has to do with healing. At the relationship level, sixth house issues would concern joint projects and activities, and the kinds of services that can be better performed by two rather than by one individual. The partnership will be looking at the areas in which they are required to work together in a day-to-day, routine manner.

SEVENTH HOUSE

The seventh house has to do with partnership issues, either personal or professional, and on a spiritual level, the marriage between soul and personality. Anything related to this house can have a very important influence on the topic of this book, namely how people relate, since the seventh house deals with close personal relationships, and it is only in close relationships that the kinds of karmic difficulties we are dealing with.

EIGHTH HOUSE

The eighth house concerns issues of death and transformation. Partnerships influenced by this house will probably, at some point, be required to go through a major transformation in order to achieve the needed growth. As a result, partnerships with the eighth house prominent will probably be very dramatic in their development. This house also deals with joint finances, and so money and the use of money may be at issue and the lesson of the partnership may be to learn to work with others when handling funds, or to use joint funds for a higher, spiritual purpose.

NINTH HOUSE

The ninth house deals with our spiritual values, our philosophies and moral code. Hence, it is related to higher learning for through education we develop our moral values and religious philosophies. This is also the reason that the ninth house is related to travel; through learning from cultures different from our own, we broaden our horizons. In a relationship, ninth house emphasis can mean on one level that the two of you will be involved in travel or learning or higher education, and on a higher level, it can mean that you are somehow involved in the development of each others moral and spiritual value systems.

TENTH HOUSE

Since the tenth house is related to career, status and standing in the world, the tenth house in relationships has somehow to deal with the status of the two of you, or what one person brings to the other's person's status or career. The tenth house can also be related to authority and authority figures, and on a higher level, your spiritual teachers, so the relationship could be one of power, status and authority, or one person in the relationship could wield some kind of authoritative power over the other person.

ELEVENTH HOUSE

The eleventh house is related to friends and groups, and hopes and wishes, and your spiritual aspirations, so its connection to relationships can be easily seen. If this house is prominent in a relationship, the two people may share the same friends and/or be active in the same organizations, or they may have difficulties to resolve regarding friends and associates. Also, they may have similar hopes, wishes and aspirations or may be learning to adjust or their hopes and wishes so as to perform better as a partnership.

TWELFTH HOUSE

The twelfth house is the house of hidden or behind the scenes issues. It can house our hidden treasures as well as our hidden psychological or subconscious issues. The twelfth house is also related to sacrifice and selfless service to others, and imprisonment. The prisons can be real prisons or prisons of our own making. In a relationship, twelfth house issues usually relate to something hidden or behind the scenes, for instance a clandestine romance. But it can just as easily relate to relationships that we feel are imprisoning in some way, or where one or both of the individuals is required to sacrifice in some way.

Astrology & Difficult Relationships: WHY ARE YOU IN MY LIFE?

ASPECTS

CONJUNCTION

The conjunction is the most powerful of the aspects. It occurs when two planets, or a planet and an angle, or two angles, are located at the same degree. The result is that the energies of both planets or angles are combined, thus giving the relationship a more potent effect than the energies alone would have. The word "power" is used here because this is an explosion of energies, and so the result is not always a peaceful and smooth combination; depending on the nature of the planets involved and the level of development of the individuals, the energy of the conjunction can be used for either powerfully positive or powerfully negative effects.

OPPOSITION

The opposition is almost as powerful as the conjunction. It represents a 180 degree relationship between planets and/or angles, and has the potential to be turned into a conjunction if the two energies can be combined in such a way that each is respected. If there is no meeting of the forces, then it can be very disruptive, for the energies are at odds with each other. The opposition requires compromise; a way must be found to balance the two energies.

SQUARE

The square is a 90 degree relationship between the planets and/or angles. A square indicates that there is something standing in the way and until the obstacle is cleared away, the two energies cannot work together as they should. The square can be turned into a positive flow of energy between the two planets if the necessary work is done to clear away the obstacle. This requires first recognizing the obstacle, and to do this, each person must look inside him self.

TRINE

With a trine, the planets and/or angles are 120 degrees apart. The trine indicates a smooth flowing of the energies between the planets or angles, so the energy is easy to work with and can be used without any effort on the part of the individuals involved.

SEXTILE

A sextile represents a 60 degree relationship between planets and/or angles. The operation of a sextile is similar to that of a trine, only not quite as accessible. Whereas with the trine, everything just flows naturally, with the sextile, some effort is required on the part of the individuals involved if the ideal energy flow is to be achieved. Therefore it is usually said that the sextile offers the "opportunity" for a free flow of energy. It is up to you to take the opportunity or it will be wasted.

INCONJUNCT (QUINQUNX)

An inconjunct or quinqunx relationship exists between two planets and/or angles when the degree of separation is 150 degrees. An inconjunct has often been described as one creating frustration, mainly because it indicates that there is something amiss in the relationship and that a minor adjustment of some sort is required. The frustration results if no attempt is made to figure out the required adjustment and then make it. Inconjuncts, just like squares can be made to work if we can figure out what is wrong and then take the necessary steps to fix it.

CHAPTER THREE

CATEGORIZING DIFFICULT RELATIONSHIPS

Now that we've taken care of all the preliminary issues and agree on our definitions, we are ready to get to the heart of this subject. We learned in Chapter One how to define a difficult relationship. In this chapter, we're going to identify and categorize these difficult relationships, and talk about why these difficult people are bothering us so much, why they seem to have so much control over us, and what we can do about it. We will categorize the various types of relationships based upon the planet or angle involved, and so, in the end, we will have fifteen major categories, based upon the ten major planets, the four angles, and a special category called mirroring relationships.

When we categorize relationships, we will be looking at conjunctions only. We learned in Chapter Two that conjunctions are the most powerful of the relationships between planets or planets and angles, so of course they are the most powerful in our lives, especially in relationships. The other aspects are important and play a role in relating as you will see later on in this book, but conjunctions are the most important because they wield the most power. Difficult relationships are almost always difficult because of a difficulty in utilizing the power of a conjunction. So, as we name and categorize relationships in this chapter, we are always talking about conjunctions.

CATEGORIZING DIFFICULT RELATIONSHIPS

Let's talk a little bit more about why that should be. A conjunction is a point in space shared by the same two planets. If two individuals are each supplying one of the planets, then they are vying for power. Obviously, for a relationship to run smoothly, we cannot be constantly pushing and shoving each other to be the one on top. Some sort of combining must come about so that both the energies are equally represented, and so that both of the energies are utilized in the best possible way. This equitable combining takes place when the parties learn the role of each of the energies separately and how they can be made to work together to produce something unique. That something unique has to be better than either of the energies could produce by themselves.

CATEGORY ONE: SELF-AWARENESS (Sun)

Anytime someone has a planet conjuncting your Sun, the relationship will have to do with the development of your sense of self. What you perceive as a difficult relationship is actually a problem with the way you define yourself. If your definition of yourself were correct, then you would not have an issue with the other person, and you would be able to use their energies to help you in your creative self-expression.

What do I mean by that? Let me give you an example. When someone's Moon conjuncts your Sun and you are having a hard time relating to them, you are feeling their emotions much stronger than you should, and are letting them shift your focus from one of forward movement to an inner, emotional and reactionary response. The Sun stands out and shines brightly, for it wants to be seen; the Moon hides the brilliance of the Sun in darkness, chaining it to past memories and past emotional responses. Suppose this person with the darkening Moon is your father. You have always felt uneasy in your father's company because he always makes you "feel" like you are not living up to his standards. No matter what you do, he is never happy, so when you are around him, you always revert to the person you were as a child. The key word is "feel." These lunar feelings are holding you back, keeping you from being who you truly are. To change this situation, the first step is to recognize that these feelings are from the past, and that they no longer exist unless you step backwards to where they lie. If you move forward, they cannot touch you. Get out of the past. As for the father in this example, he needs to recognize that he is holding onto a totally outdated emotional view of who he is and what you, as a reflection of him, should be.

Your sense of who you are and where you stand in relation to the rest of the world has to be clearly developed and clearly understood before you can ever hope to achieve what it is that you came here to do. Each of us has a soul purpose, a reason for being, and if we are not able to achieve that soul purpose, then we will have failed in this incarnation. While the theory of reincarnation says that we have as many lifetimes as we need to fulfill that purpose, the sooner we can do it the better. So in every lifetime we want to grow spiritually as much as possible. Developing a true sense of who we are and being able to express that self fully is quite important to our spiritual growth. That is why when people that we consider difficult are making conjunctive aspects to our Sun, we need to pay close attention to what they are doing to or for us. We need to understand that the difficulty has arisen because we need help in achieving our self-expression. When we truly express ourselves, we are on the way to understanding who we truly are and what our special talents are. When we know who we truly are and our special talents, we can get on with whatever it is that we came here to do. When someone has a planet conjuncting our Sun, we need to understand that we have drawn that particular person into our life so that they can point out what it is we need to do in order to achieve full self-expression. The nature of the relationship in general and the person in particular

CATEGORIZING DIFFICULT RELATIONSHIPS

will show us the direction in which we need to travel, so that we can reach our full potential.

Now let's look at the other side of the coin. Suppose your Sun conjuncts a planet or angle in another person's chart. Your role is to highlight the expression of the particular planet that your Sun conjuncts. In the above example about your father's Moon conjuncting your Sun, your role in your father's life is to bring light or shed light on the functioning of his Moon so that he can better "see" where he needs to change his emotional patterns. If your Sun conjuncts someone's Mercury, then you shine light on their communicating and thinking processes, to help them clear things up in that area, and to help them excel in the area of communication. Shining your sunlight on someone's Venus would highlight their ability to love, and on their Mars, you would help them see the effects of their passions and desires. On their Uranus, you would help someone better understand their volatility issues, and you would alert them to deceptive or escapist tendencies on their Neptune. And if your Sun conjuncts their Pluto, you are showing them how they use their personal power.

CATEGORY TWO: RELEASING THE PAST (Moon)

If you are in a relationship with someone and you keep dwelling upon things that happened in the past, and you can't forget them so that the relationship can move forward, more than likely the Moon is involved. When the Moon is conjuncting a planet in someone else's chart, it is always an indication of a past life connection, or at least of something from the past. In difficult relationships, it usually means that there is something that needs to be forgiven and/or released.

The Moon's position in your chart shows the area of your life where you are clinging to the past or clinging to outdated emotional responses. The planet conjuncting your Moon shows how you can go about releasing these old emotional responses, and how the other person can help you to do that. For instance, we talked earlier about how another's Sun conjuncting your Moon has to deal with shedding light on the situation so that you can see more clearly what emotional responses are no longer relevant. Mercury conjuncting your Moon can mean that the key to releasing old emotions has to deal somehow with communication or the thinking process. Someone's Saturn conjuncting your Moon would mean that the emotional release comes through some particular responsibility or duty owed to that person.

    Your Moon is affecting the other person by bringing an emotional element to the situation, and forcing the other person to deal with the energy of their planet in an emotional way. For instance, if your Moon conjuncts their Venus, and there is a difficulty relating, the Venus person may be placing too much of a financial emphasis on the relationship, or perhaps over-emphasizing possessions and material comfort, and it is your job to bring in intuitive and emotional understanding so they can learn to express unconditional love, the higher level meaning of Venus. If your Moon conjuncts someone's Mars, your role in the relationship may be to help them take an emotional or intuitive look at their desires and their needs.

    Wherever the Moon is involved in a relationship, the past and ingrained emotional responses are being worked on, and because these are emotional issues, the process can be difficult and painful. But progress is good, and every time that you or the other party are able to release some inhibiting emotional response from the past, you are one step closer to fulfilling the purpose of the relationship.

CATEGORY THREE: PERSONALITY INTEGRATION (Mercury)

    In Roman mythology, Mercury was the link between the

gods and mortals. In layman's terms, Mercury is our link to our higher self, or soul. Mercury then, is all about personality integration, that is, the integration of the higher and lower self.

When a planet in another person's chart conjuncts your Mercury, and you have a terrible response to that person, terrible enough to consider it to be a difficult relationship, then you are relating to that person to help you become aware of the need for work in the area of personality integration. In other words, that person is irritating you because you have not successfully linked your higher and lower self, and this person is here to help you do that. The planet that conjoins Mercury will determine the method you are to use as you approach this personality integration. For instance, if it is Venus, then you are to use the approach of impersonal love; if it is Pluto, then you are to use your personal power and resolve.

An example of how this kind of relationship works is as follows. Suppose you have an uncle whose Mars conjuncts your Mercury. You have never had a good relationship with him; everything you say to him angers him. You seem to know how to hit all of his sensitive buttons, and you seem to enjoy doing it. You believe that the two of you are not on the same wavelength and that you will never be able to communicate, so you don't even try talking to him anymore. At some point, if you are serious about fixing the relationship, you need to ask yourself why he always responds so negatively to your comments. What is it about what you say that makes him so angry? Perhaps it is because you are not communicating at the higher level; perhaps you are communicating in a petty, lower level, way, and are therefore always offending him. Maybe you need to think a little more before you speak, try to connect with your higher self which would not allow you to think mean thoughts, nor to say mean things to others. Mercury makes us aware of both our selves. The proper way for this relationship to work, from your point of view, is for your uncle to be the one who sounds the whistle when you are ignoring your other, higher self, so you should thank him for it. Rather than seeing him as a difficult person in your life, realize that he is an aid in your soul growth, and appreciate the fact that he makes you think before you speak. In order to change the relationship from a difficult one to a smooth functioning one, you have to make some changes in the way you communicate things, but on a deeper level, you have to change the way you see and think about things. And in order to do that, you have to look higher.

From your uncle's point of view, you are someone who is hard to talk to because you are always taking the fun out of life. By constantly being the rational, thoughtful person, you are "cooling" off his passions and desires. Realize that it is your role in the relationship to help your uncle see in a rational way where he is letting his desires and passions control his actions.

Both of you are helping each other, he as the Mars person forces you to think before you speak and to speak from higher levels, and you as the Mercury person are showing him how to bring an element of rationality to his actions.

CATEGORY FOUR: UNCONDITIONAL LOVE (Venus)

If your Venus conjuncts a planet in someone else's chart, you are to learn from that person how to love unconditionally, and then, by example, you are to teach them how to do the same thing. We are to love each other simply because we are all part of the human family, and if you are in a difficult relationship with someone who has a planet touching your Venus, then you have to learn that lesson. We are all different, and we may run into people who are wired so differently from us that we cannot figure out a way to relate to them at all, and more importantly, we sometimes don't even see a need to relate at all.

We can go through many lifetimes never touching others, or isolating ourselves from those who are "different" from us. If your Venus touches someone, then you are to love them unconditionally, because they are in your life and you can do nothing about it. So if you choose to isolate yourself from them, to allow hatreds and ill feelings to enter into the relationship, then you will be miserable. The only thing you can do to end the misery is to release all of the preconceived notions you may have about them, and just love them. I am not referring to the emotional, gushy type of love we see in the movies. I am referring to a higher kind of love. Love them with a love that is intelligent. Love them with a love that is all-inclusive and all-accepting, for we are all part of the same humanity, and therefore all connected.

If you are the one with the Venus, then recognize that the other person may feel that you are someone they will never accept, or you may be totally repulsive to them, and so they do all they can to avoid you. As the Venus person, you should be big enough to handle that outcome for you should understand that love takes time. Regardless of how they feel about you, you should still set the example by continuing to love them and you should never stop. Let the person know that the olive branch is always being stretched out and will be there whenever they wish to grab it.

If the other person is the Venus person, then understand that you are learning about love from them, and that your planet will show you how. For instance, if your Pluto conjuncts their Venus, then you are learning to temper your willpower and intensity with love. If you Saturn conjuncts their Venus, then you are learning how to manifest things, which Saturn does so well, but with love as the underlying motivation. Each planet has its own objective, and coupled with Venus, that objective is always qualified by love.

CATEGORY FIVE: TRANSFORMATION OF DESIRES (Mars)

If you are the Mars person, then this relationship is

Astrology & Difficult Relationships: WHY ARE YOU IN MY LIFE?

helping you to identify and eliminate unacceptable desires and passions. And depending upon how strongly you desire these things, you will find the relationship more or less difficult. If you are obsessed with having something or someone, then of course you are going to be furious with the person who you perceive as standing in the way of your getting what you want.

Since the conjunction is the most powerful of the aspects, this power, where Mars is concerned, may push a person towards overly aggressive or even violent behavior. If you are the Mars person and you are becoming violent or extremely aggressive towards the other person because you can't get what you want, then shame on you. Violence is never a solution; if your desires are not being met, then you need to take a good look at your desires and see if they need to be changed.

If you aren't clear as to what desires you need to address, take a look at the planet conjuncting your Mars. For instance, if it is the Sun, the issues may be related to how you express yourself; if it is the Moon, there may be strong desires related to the past or to emotional reactions that need to be overcome; if the other planet is Mercury, the desires could be related to communicating problems, or to faulty thinking.

On the other side of the coin, if someone's Mars is conjuncting a planet in your chart, then your role is to help them use their Martian energy is a positive way, and to help them see areas where they are letting their lower level desires and passions take control.

To work positively in a relationship, Martian energy should provide the impetus and vitality to pursue some combined cause or objective. Look at the other planet in the conjunction to determine what the real objective of the relationship should be, make the necessary adjustments, and then you will find that the relationship has all of the energy it needs to make it successful. Instead of using your Martian energy to selfishly go after only what you want, think about how you can use it to pursue something

CATEGORIZING DIFFICULT RELATIONSHIPS

beneficial to the both of you.

CATEGORY SIX: TEACHER/PUPIL (Jupiter)

In relationships, Jupiter often represents the teacher, so whoever has the Jupiter in the relationship is the teacher, and the other person the pupil. Jupiter expands or broadens or horizons, or takes us to a higher level of consciousness, so if you don't want to learn or to expand or to go to a higher state of understanding, then you will have problems with this person.

This teacher/pupil relationship can manifest itself in many ways. For instance, someone with Jupiter conjunct Pluto in another's chart will find that his purpose in the relationship is to help the other person expand his concept of what power is and how it is to be used. If the other planet were Neptune, the Jupiter person would be there to increase or broaden the person's spiritual understanding of himself. In a difficult relationship, Jupiter on the Ascendant of another person would be an indication that you, the Jupiter person, would aid in the elevation of consciousness of the other person, and also in their ability to achieve their soul purpose.

It is quite common to see a mother's Jupiter conjunct the Ascendant of her child. One way to interpret this is that the mother expanded the child's state of consciousness by being the vehicle that brought him from the plane of the unborn to that of the living. If this conjunction is present in a difficult relationship between a mother and child, then the child may resent the mother for the state of his life, or may blame the mother for his problems in dealing with his life. Obviously, that would be an instance where the child needs to learn to embrace his life and to celebrate his time on the physical plane and use it wisely.

If you are the Jupiter person, realize that you have something that you can teach the other person, or something that

Astrology & Difficult Relationships: WHY ARE YOU IN MY LIFE?

you can share that will uplift them or take them to a higher level. So don't be stingy with your efforts. Jupiter is big and expansive, and that is how you should behave in the relationship. You should be generous and full of optimism and joy as you endeavor to bring the other person along.

If another person's Jupiter conjuncts a planet in your chart, then realize that there are things that you can learn from them, and rather than fighting with them, appreciate the fact that they are there, endeavor to learn what they can teach you, and be thankful for the opportunity. The Jupiter person brings knowledge to you, expands your understanding and your abilities. They allow you to express the qualities of your planet is a bigger way.

CATEGORY SEVEN: DEBTOR/DEBTEE (Saturn)

This is just as the name implies. One person owes a debt to the other, or has a responsibility to or for the other person. This implies a karmic relationship, and so naturally, Saturn is the planet most often seen in this type of relationship. If someone's Saturn conjuncts a planet in your chart, you may owe that person something that must be repaid, or you may have a major responsibility that must be fulfilled for that person's benefit. If the relationship is difficult, maybe you are not living up to your responsibility or you have not yet paid your debt and therefore you feel as if they are restricting or limiting your choices.

Having Saturn conjunct a planet in your chart doesn't necessarily imply that you have done something bad to them in this or a past life. You may have decided to assume this responsibility as an opportunity for personal growth. For instance, we bring children into the world for many reasons, a major Saturn responsibility, and sometimes it is to learn how to love unconditionally, or how to care for others. The most important thing to remember about a Saturn relationship is that unless and until the obligation or responsibility is fulfilled, or the correct choice is made, the relationship will not go the way you want it to go, so the most obvious plan of action is to do what is required so that you can free yourself and move on.

If someone's Saturn conjuncts a planet in your chart and you experience that person as someone who is limiting your options, understand that they are there to teach you discipline and responsibility. For example, suppose you are constantly fighting with your mother-in-law. You compare your astrological charts and determine that her Saturn conjoins your Mars. You feel that she never lets you do anything you want to do and that she is always against you. Realize that she, as the debtee, is attempting, through her behavior, to show you what responsibility looks like, which is her role in the relationship. She may not be doing it in the most effective way, and you may need to show her how to change her behavior a bit to achieve the desired result. But whether you are the debtor or the debtee, Saturn will make it quite clear that it is only through the fulfilling of our responsibilities that the relationship will progress and manifest as it should.

CATEGORY EIGHT: IMPETUS OF CHANGE (Uranus)

If your Uranus conjuncts a planet in another person's chart, understand that your role is to be the impetus of change in that person's life, and expect the other person not to like it sometimes. Knowing that that is your role will help you to understand why you have to do the things that you do, and that you are not doing them frivolously. The person really does need you to shake up their life every now and then. If the other person dislikes you for this, though, you will have to figure out a way to make him see that what you are doing is really beneficial. The way to approach this is to identify the planet that Uranus conjuncts in his or her chart and that will show you how the other person views your actions. If Venus is the planet, for example, you may be viewed as someone who interferes with his love life. If the Sun is the other planet, you may be viewed as always trying to throw water on that person's ability to express his true self.

Turning the tables, if someone is always shaking up your life, making you do things that you don't want to do, things that you feel you are not ready to do, and you dislike them for it, more than likely Uranus is involved. If anyone's Uranus conjuncts a planet or angle in your chart, that person will always be an impetus of change in your life. Accept that and appreciate what it is that they are doing for you. Recognize that whenever you are stuck in a holding pattern in your life, you need this person to come in and shatter your old views, values, etc., so that you can move on. Change is difficult sometimes, but usually only if we fight it. Change is necessary, and if you learn to embrace change, you can learn to embrace this person and thus put the relationship on a different footing.

CATEGORY NINE: REALITY CHECK (Neptune)

If your Neptune is conjuncting a planet in someone's chart and the relationship is difficult, realize that they may see you as someone who is deceptive, delusional, or someone who engages in addictive behavior. The key to improving these relationships is to separate the unreal from the real. Reality can be much more beautiful than fantasy.

If you are in a difficult relationship with someone whose Neptune conjuncts one of your planets, the Neptune person is here to help you "dissolve" unrealistic, delusional, or addictive attitudes, people, etc., from your life. They are here to force you to "get real" about your life, so that you can connect with the truth of who you are.

Sometimes this Neptune person can have a truly

detrimental effect on you and can bring you to your lowest of lows. At the very worst, these are the people who will help you support a drug habit or some other addiction. At the very best, though, these people can help you to see the highest and most beautiful aspect of a person, a relationship, a situation, etc. Since we are dealing with difficult relationships here, more than likely we are dealing with Neptune functioning in a negative fashion, and the task for us is to figure out the negative function of Neptune and turn it into a positive one.

For instance, you may have a friend who you know is no good for you and yet you cannot break the connection. You may not have reached the point where you even consider it a difficult relationship; you may only see this person as a friend. Still, you know that you always get into trouble when you are with this person, for when you are with them, your view of reality shifts and you see things as being okay when in fact they are not. When you are with this friend, it is okay to drink too much, or overeat, or worse, do drugs. At some point, though, you will begin to realize that if you ever want to overcome these addictions, you are going to have to sever the relationship, or at least change its nature.

Wherever Neptune is involved, we are asked to see the ideal, the highest, and so you are being asked to see yourself in the highest light possible. So, if someone's Neptune is conjuncting a planet in your chart and you consider this person to be difficult, then this relationship is about separating delusions from reality.

CATEGORY TEN: CONTROL & POWER ISSUES (Pluto)

Pluto, the last of the outer planets, uses as its modus operandi, personal power. In a difficult relationship where Pluto is involved, the problem almost always has to do with control issues and power struggles. If your Pluto is conjuncting a planet is someone's chart and the relationship is difficult, then they see you as controlling or wanting power. It is your obligation in the relationship to use your personal power to help them intensify the lesson of the planet your Pluto conjuncts. If you are not doing that, then you are indeed using power incorrectly and creating the difficulty in the relationship. Ask yourself what you are doing that is giving them the impression that you are trying to control them. Be honest. Are you trying to control them because you don't have control of your own life? Are you trying to live vicariously through them?

If someone's Pluto conjuncts a planet in your chart and you consider that person to be a difficult person, then that person wants control over you or some area of your life. By looking at the house and sign involved, you can tell where their interests lie. So if someone is trying to control you, usually it is because they are lacking in that area and erroneously believe that by controlling your life in that area, they are fixing their own. People with control issues usually do not ever take a long look at their own lives and try to fix them. They live vicariously through others, and so as long as you are doing what they want you to do, they feel successful.

For instance, you may have a friend who was a bully in school, and now as an adult, is still bullying you, only not physically. He is running your life. He advises you on who you should go out with, what jobs you should accept, where you should live, etc. The power that this person wields is being used in a negative fashion. The correct way to wield this power in a relationship is to use it towards the objective of the planet of the other person. If, in this example, Pluto conjuncts your Moon, then the correct use of this power is to help you rid yourself of outdated emotional responses and habits.

But if you are the Moon person, how do you get to the point where the Pluto person is using his power to help you rather than control you? One way is to deflect their power back on themselves whenever they are using it negatively and then give them a positive way to utilize the energy. Going back to the high school bully turned architect of your life, the next time he suggests that you do something, tell him that's a good idea, he should do it himself. If he suggests that you move to a certain neighborhood, tell him that he really would enjoy living there. Hopefully they will realize that they are using their power in the wrong way. And when that moment happens, then you can feel free to call upon them again, to use their power in a way that is productive for both of you, and that will depend upon what planet their Pluto conjuncts in your chart. If it is Venus, for instance, they would make an excellent partner in learning about and giving unconditional love, for the two of you together would make an intensely loving pair.

CATEGORY ELEVEN: CONSCIOUSNESS (Ascendant)

Anytime a planet or angle in another person's chart touches your Ascendant, there is a strong connection between the two of you. If you consider the relationship difficult, sit down for you are in for a shock. The other person is here to assist you in achieving your life purpose, so no matter how you feel about this person, there are major lessons to be learned from him or her. As discussed earlier, the Ascendant represents those qualities or traits that you are supposed to be developing and using in this lifetime because they represent the direction that your soul wants you to take. Therefore, anyone connected with your Ascendant has to help you in some way to develop these traits or characteristics.

If someone's Mercury conjuncts your Ascendant, and you have difficulty relating to them, perhaps they are trying to teach you how to be more rational if you are to achieve your soul purpose. Or if it is Venus, you need to learn to love unconditionally before you can succeed in your Ascendant's goal. Achieving one's soul purpose requires a kind of consciousness awakening or expansion, and the qualities of the planet that the other person brings to your Ascendant will allow you to make the transition to that higher state of consciousness so that you can fully display your soul qualities.

If one of your planets conjuncts someone's Ascendant, and you and that person have difficulties relating, then realize that you have a definite role to play in helping them to raise their level of soul recognition or soul consciousness, and they are probably fighting your help. With such an important role, you have to continue the effort, although you may have to soften your approach a bit. But keep at it for the help you are giving to them is invaluable.

CATEGORY TWELVE: YOUR NEGATIVE TRAITS (Descendant)

If your Descendant conjuncts a planet in someone's chart, and the relationship is difficult, you are being shown those traits or characteristics that are buried in you that you need to deal with. You are being forced to recognize that these traits exist in you, and how your relationship develops is an indication of how well you are assimilating those characteristics. Since we are talking about difficult relationships here, obviously you are not assimilating them very well.

Here is an example of how this may work in a difficult relationship. Suppose your Descendant conjuncts Saturn in the other person's chart. Saturn, we know, can have the effect of restricting or limiting our actions. We can't do what we want to do; we have to be very focused and very serious when this person is around. Perhaps this Saturn person is showing us that we need to be more responsible, that our other self is very irresponsible, or lazy, or unfocused. Suppose the planet conjuncting your Descendant is Mars. Mars has to do with desires and the energy and drive and vitality to pursue them. When you are with this Mars person, you become wildly aggressive. You can't understand why this person awakens those feelings in you. But the lesson here is that you need to look inside yourself, for those wildly aggressive and passionate feelings are lurking beneath the surface.

If the shoe is on the other foot, that is, if you are the person whose planet conjuncts the Descendant of another, every time you are together, the other person reacts negatively because your very presence forces them to deal with issues within themselves, although they probably don't realize that these issues are coming from themselves. They are blaming them totally on you. In that case, you may have to soften your approach to that person, until they gradually realize that the difficulties lie in themselves and not in you. Once that happens, the relationship should improve.

CATEGORY THIRTEEN: YOUR FOUNDATION (Nadir)

The Nadir is the bottom of the chart, the base or foundation. So when a planet in someone else's chart touches your Nadir, or foundation, and the relationship is troubling, you are shaken to the core. It's like being on the twentieth floor of a building when someone begins pulling out bricks in the basement. We want our lives to be stable, and this person is causing the foundation of our life to wobble.

The thing to do here is to look at the planet that is causing the wobbling. Pluto, for instance, would be trying to totally transform your foundation, and this is difficult unless you can figure out the reason why a drastic transformation is needed in your life. Uranus will have a similar, disruptive effect, and you will not like the person unless you again learn to embrace change and understand the reason for it.

If Mercury is the offending planet, the other person is causing your foundation to wobble because of irrational communication and an unstable intellectual foundation. If the Moon is involved, maybe your emotional base is just too emotional and needs overhauling. Or, if Venus is the planet on your Nadir, perhaps your basic emotional or psychological nature needs to be a little more loving, or to express more beauty in your life.

If you are the person responsible for the wobbling, that is, if you have a planet conjoining someone's Nadir, know that your mere presence is causing a major structural change in their life, and that is the cause of the difficulty between the two of you. You must show the other person that you are not a threat, why the changes are necessary and that you are there to help them.

CATEGORY FOURTEEN: YOUR WORLD STATUS (Midheaven)

Whenever a planet or angle in another's chart touches your Midheaven, they will be influential in your career, or whatever it is you are putting out into the world. If the aspects were trines and sextiles, that would mean that this person was going to beneficial and helpful in most cases. However, since we are talking about difficult relationships, and we are focusing on conjunctions, then the other person may be doing things that we interpret as standing in our way, or creating problems for us in our career or profession.

Two can do much more than just one, and the correct way of looking at this person is how they can help you to put your best foot forward. For instance, if the other person's Sun conjuncts your Midheaven, they will be able to help you to become known in your area of expertise. They will "advertise" your skills. So the question, then, is why do you feel that they are difficult? Maybe its because you don't want the publicity, and they are here to force you out of the shadows into the light.

Reversing the situation, suppose it is your Sun that is conjuncting another's Midheaven and they see you as pressuring them to step into the spotlight when they are not ready, or they see you as a nuisance. Realize that your Sun is there to help their career, so you have to figure out how to do it in a non-threatening, beneficial way and a way that will be accepted by the other person.

CATEGORIZING DIFFICULT RELATIONSHIPS

CATEGORY FIFTEEN: MIRRORING RELATIONSHIPS

The purpose of a mirroring relationship is for the two people to help each other overcome bad habits or incorrect physical, emotional or mental faults by displaying those traits so that the other person can recognize them. The astrological definition of a mirroring relationship is when a planet in your chart conjuncts the same planet in another's chart. (You want to look only at the inner, personal planets. The outer planets, Uranus, Neptune and Pluto, are generational and so anyone near your age will have those planets conjunct yours.)

The reason that mirroring relationships can be so challenging is because we are always the last to recognize our own negative habits, and so when we see then played out by someone else, our response is usually to see what needs to be corrected in the other person, but not see it in ourselves. The more closely another person resembles us, the more we tend to dislike that person. Mirroring relationships can help us make tremendous strides in our personal growth if we can finally realize what they are.

For instance, if you and your sister have your Moons conjunct, and you have difficulties relating, you are mirroring to each other negative emotional habits. If your Mars conjuncts another person's Mars and you are having difficulties getting along, issues relating to the appropriate use of energy and aggression are being mirrored to each other. Once you recognize what is happening with your mirroring relationship, you can begin to make positive changes, and the two of you can begin to improve your relationship.

So there you have it. You now know the major categories of and reasons for relationships. But before you begin looking at your own relationships, there are some other issues that need to be considered and we will look at them in the next few chapters.

CHAPTER FOUR

IF THE RELATIONSHIP IS UNBEARABLE

Let's say that you have successfully categorized your relationships, have been able to make some sense of them and better understand why you are in them. There is one small problem, though. You find that dealing with the person is so emotionally painful that you just cannot bring yourself to do the things that you need to do to improve the relationship. The pain you feel may be quite noticeable to others, or it may be hidden, but it is there nonetheless, and it is keeping you from moving forward in your relationship.

Whenever we are dealing with pain in relationships, we are usually talking about strong emotional reactions, and so more than likely, the water signs, Cancer, Scorpio and Pisces, play a large role. The person feeling the pain may have the Sun sign or Ascendant in a water sign, or perhaps he has a stellium of planets in a water element.

But it is not just the water signs that cause painful relationships. The earth signs are also very sensitive. I can hear you saying no, but think about it. The earth signs are the opposite poles of the water signs, so they deal with the same issues; they just handle them in a different way. An earth sign person can be just as hurt, but will bury that pain in the "earth" so that we cannot see it unless we really dig for it. They will tell you that their feelings aren't hurt and yet they may be dying inside. They can appear to be totally detached, when in actuality they have simply hidden their emotional responses.

Pain has a purpose, and burying it will not allow you to learn that purpose. Therefore, when advising people on how to deal with the hurt of relationships so that they can move forward to fix them, we need to look at both poles of the emotional scale, expressed and hidden emotions. Therefore, we will look at both ends of the spectrum by analyzing Cancer and Capricorn together, Taurus and Scorpio together, and Pisces and Virgo together. With the water signs, the goal is to turn extreme emotionalism into detached sensitivity. With the earth signs, the goal is to unearth their buried emotions, transform them into sensitivity, and then deal with them in an appropriate way.

CANCER

The water sign of Cancer can be extremely emotional and sensitive, and would rather stay hidden away in its shell than deal with rude, obnoxious, or just plain mean and unpleasant people. Cancers know this about themselves, and so they are always slow to open up to others. They have to wait until they feel very comfortable with them. Anyone with a lot of Cancerian energy in his or her make-up is usually very reserved. But just like their namesake, the crab, they are also very tenacious. Once their claws get hold of something, they refuse to let it go. Many times this is cited as a negative characteristic of Cancers, that they cling to the past, or to outmoded or outdated versions of themselves. And while holding onto something that needs to be replaced is unwise, tenacity in and of itself can be a very good quality to have.

Tenacity is related to determination, and if a Cancer person can use his tenacity or determination in a positive way, he can

Astrology & Difficult Relationships: WHY ARE YOU IN MY LIFE?

accomplish much, including holding together a difficult relationship even though it may be painful. The only way for a Cancer person to deal with the pain is to turn the focus away from the emotional level of the relationship and focus only on the rational or mental level. If you can stay focused at the mental level, then you are more likely to develop the emotional detachment so necessary to carry on in an otherwise painful relationship. Emotional pain is not felt at the mental or rational level. It is looked upon rationally, and in that way is turned into detached sensitivity.

A very emotional Cancer person needs to learn how to "turn on" the mental side and shut down the emotional side at will, so that whenever it is time to deal with that particular relationship, it can be done without any of the negative emotional feelings such as guilt, sorrow, hurt, jealousy, etc. An easy way to do this is to think of a mental picture that will always take you to that mental place, so that you can call upon it every time you feel yourself falling into the emotional trap door. Work on developing this mental picture when you are not feeling very emotional, and practice calling it up so that you can do it at will.

For instance, you might choose as your mental picture a vision of yourself accepting a Nobel Prize for science. Think about how smart and how mentally focused you would have to be to win a Nobel Prize for science. Add as much detail as you like. The more detail, the more real it will become in your mind. If you are good at visualization, this will be quite easy for you. If not, you will have to work on it a bit but you can do it. The purpose of this exercise is structure in your mind a new concept of yourself that can be called upon whenever you need it.

So, at the next family holiday when you are forced to confront your dreaded aunt or uncle or cousin, or whoever is the difficult person in your life, rather than feigning illness so that you don't have to face them, call upon your master vision and let it lift you out of yourself. If the difficult person tries to start an argument with you, respond not as yourself but as the person in your master vision. The Nobel Prize winning scientist, for instance, would simply laugh at your cousin when he insulted you, and walk away.

If visualizations don't work for you, another way to lift yourself out of the emotional realm is through the repetition of mantras. Mantras are words, phrases, or sentences that are repeated over and over again until gradually, their meaning becomes ingrained in our personality. A mantra for an overly-emotional Cancer person might be, "I will not react emotionally. I will interpret everything through the lens of the mind." Take your time and develop the mantra that works for you and then use it.

CAPRICORN

Now let's look at the other end of the spectrum, Capricorn. If you have a lot of Capricorn energy in your nature, you are most likely known for your dignified and even taciturn manner. You would never let your emotions show. This is because you, above all others, understand that life isn't supposed to be easy. It is supposed to be hard work and those who do the required work are rewarded, and those who don't, lose. You don't cry about your circumstances or feel sorry for yourself. You do what you know you are required to do, and you do it without complaining.

Trouble is, sometimes you do have things happen to you that legitimately cause you to want to cry or feel sorry for yourself, and you hide those feelings away. While emotional detachment is one of your strengths, false detachment can be your downfall. If you are truly hurting and are not admitting it and not allowing it to be handled in the proper way, you are setting yourself up for a multitude of personal problems. Anytime we bury our feelings, they have to find a way to be released, and so they can surface in some very strange and unhealthy ways. Everyone has emotions, but some of us know how to control them and some of us don't. The way to control them is not to bury them. The way to

Astrology & Difficult Relationships: WHY ARE YOU IN MY LIFE?

control them is to recognize emotions for what they are, and then put them in their proper place, under the control of our rational or mental self.

Burying emotions is sometimes true of all the earth signs, but the way to uncover them differs slightly for each earth sign. In the case of Capricorn, uncovering emotions so that they can be dealt with requires giving yourself permission to be human, to feel. Capricorns can sometimes become so enmeshed in following the conventions and doing what's right that they lose themselves altogether in conventionality. Appearances become more important than reality.

If a Capricorn person is involved in a difficult relationship and the relationship is too painful for them to deal with, they will simply, without any emotion, avoid the person and the entire situation. They don't have a shell like their Cancer opposites, but they do have their own outer crust, a crust so thick and hard that not even a trickle of their true feelings shows through. Saturn rules Capricorn, and Saturn makes things concrete. So the Capricorn person has to break through the concrete, let the emotions out, and then put them in the proper place. Breaking through concrete usually requires a jackhammer. It makes a lot of noise and a lot of mess before the job is finally completed. The jackhammer is therefore a perfect visualization tool for someone wanting to reach their buried emotions.

Once the Capricorn has successfully jack hammered through the concrete and reached the level of emotions, then he can follow the advice given to his opposite sign, Cancer, as far as what to do with them. He can use visualization techniques to help him lift his emotions to the mental plane, which should be a fairly simple thing for him to do since he is already detached by nature, due to his more rational approach to relating. Once the Capricorn person has added an emotional coloring to his already detached nature, he will have reached the level of detached sensitivity, so that he can show sensitivity in the relationship, but he will not be

IF THE RELATIONSHIP IS UNBEARABLE

ruled by his emotions and thus not be hurt.

Again, if visualization techniques do not work for you, try using mantras. Words of power, repeated over and over again, can accomplish the same thing. A possible mantra for a Capricorn person might be, "I will think through my heart."

The next pairing is Scorpio and Taurus.

SCORPIO

Scorpios are another of the water signs, and are thus prone to quite a lot of emotional responses in relationships. Their emotional base is very different from that of Cancer. Of the three water signs, Scorpios are the most likely to experience every difficult situation as a personal attack. Their strong emotional response stems from their tendency to see life as a constant battle, believing they can trust no one. This accounts for their renowned strategic abilities; they are always fighting a war. The more emotional the person, the more real the battle will seem to him. The Scorpio person is so emotionally charged that when dealing with others in general they are on their guard, but when dealing with someone in a difficult relationship, they behave as if they are facing their greatest enemy and that all of their resources are necessary to win the fight. If the Scorpio person allows his emotions to take hold, they will, like their namesake, hide under a rock until the opportune moment to "sting" the other person, hoping that the sting will send the enemy away forever.

Unfortunately, in a difficult relationship, the other person doesn't go away. That's one of the reasons that the relationship is classified as difficult. So the normal procedure for avoiding the pain of the relationship will not work here. No matter how hard you sting and how poisonous you make the venom, the person is still there. A dreaded mother-in-law, a vicious co-worker, they are in your life for the long term, so a new approach is needed.

Astrology & Difficult Relationships: WHY ARE YOU IN MY LIFE?

One of the best things for a Scorpio to do in a painfully difficult relationship is to retrain his ability to assess a situation. Every time the "enemy" says something you consider to be an attack, you must tell yourself that he is not attacking you personally. (Even if he is, don't allow yourself to believe it, for the sake of the relationship). One way to do this is to envision this person as weakened or greatly reduced in power, so that they are no threat to you. For instance, you might imagine your sarcastic uncle's words as bubbles floating out of his mouth and bursting well before they reach you. Or whenever he starts talking, you might visualize him as a cartoon character, no one that you would take seriously. You can get really good at this if you try, and you will eventually find that the words he says just melt away, and instead of seeing daggers, you just see a silly man.

If you're not good at visualization, you might try devising a mantra that can be repeated mentally whenever you feel yourself thinking negative thoughts. The point is that we are trying to find a way to take the perception of a personal attack out of the picture, so that you do not automatically respond emotionally and defensively. If you can find a way to weaken the enemy in your eyes, then there is no reason to fight, and then you can start looking for a rational way to relate.

TAURUS

As the opposite sign of Scorpio, Taurus can also be known to personalize emotions, only they are personalized towards wants and desires. As a result, an overly emotional Taurus person in a difficult relationship is apt to see the other person as an obstacle standing in the way of the Taurus person's desires, and this can be so painful that the Taurean refuses to deal with the other person. What the Taurus person should do instead is change his desires into something that would be good for both people, then he can stop feeling that the other person is standing in the way of the

IF THE RELATIONSHIP IS UNBEARABLE

things he wants. Both visualization and mantra type exercises can work here as well, and so here are some suggestions.

Before visualization can begin, you first need to identify those desires that you feel are being threatened by the other person. Once you have identified them, you can then work on enlarging them so they become more inclusive. For instance, you may be going through a divorce proceeding and are fighting over custody of your child. You want total custody and so does your wife, so you perceive her as standing in the way of what you want. Or, perhaps you are an employee and covet a promotion, and a co-worker also wants the same promotion, therefore standing in the way of your getting what you want.

These are merely examples of the kinds of desires and wishes that can be at the center of difficult relationships. Sometimes it is not very easy to pinpoint the nature of the desire that you feel is being blocked and you may have to think about it for a while. Sometimes we delude ourselves into thinking that our desires are not desires but are instead naturally due us. If the employee in the example above naturally expects that he should receive the promotion, he will have a hard time recognizing the role of his desires in the relationship with his competition. The employee, if asked about the situation, will tell you that he doesn't know why the other person does not like him. The employee doesn't see himself as being difficult; the other person is the difficult one.

The lesson here for a Taurus person is to really look at your difficult relationship and try to uncover what it is that you perceive, either consciously or unconsciously, as being threatened by the other person. The sooner you can identify the issue, the sooner you can figure out how to transform that desire into something that will benefit the both of you.

Once you have identified the issue, you can do some visualization work to help raise the desire to a higher level. You might try visualizing your desire as a seed. See yourself planting the seed and then watch it grow. You should visualize your plant growing up and out and not down. As your plant is growing up and out, see your initial desire also growing up and out. Symbolically pull one of the leaves and see what it represents. If you have done this visualization correctly, your leaf should represent something more than the original desire, and should be of a higher and healthier nature. Going back to the employee who wanted the promotion, the leaf selected from high up on the plant could correspond with his desired place in the company later on in the future. He could see the leaf as representing his commitment to the company, to the employees and to the goals of the company, a much larger and more inclusive desire than before. From that vantage point, he could see how one small promotion would not hold him back from achieving his higher goal, that of commitment to the company, and that if the other person is as committed as he, then whoever receives the promotion would be fine for the company.

The angry spouse in the child custody battle could pull a leaf from high up on the plant and see that it represented the opportunities afforded to the child by joint custody that he could not provide alone. He would recognize that by sharing custody, he would still be able to love the child, he would still be involved in the child's life, and that the more loving people in the child's life, the better. His would come to the realization that his wish of sole custody should be substituted with a wish for the best possible outcome for the child.

For those of you who prefer the power of words and thoughts, a possible mantra to help you raise your desire to a higher level might be, "I wish the best possible outcome for everyone involved." Or, "I wish to be inclusive, not exclusive." You can tailor the mantra to your own needs, but you get the idea. Once you can internalize this newer, more inclusive and higher desire, you will see that the pain of the relationship will subside.

Now we will look at the last combination, Pisces and Virgo.

IF THE RELATIONSHIP IS UNBEARABLE

PISCES

With Pisces, the problem that can sometimes arise in very painful relationships is that the Pisces person will empathize with everyone involved and will therefore feel everyone's pain. When this happens, the Pisces person just wants to shut himself off in his own dream world far from everyone to avoid having to deal with all of these feelings.

In a difficult relationship, the Pisces person needs to find a way to shut off the other person's emotions so that he can deal only with what he is feeling. And then, like the Cancer person, he must lift himself out of his emotions into a higher level. The first step is the toughest, and so needs to be addressed first.

One way for a Pisces person to learn to shut out the emotions of others is again with visualization. He needs to visualize his jangled emotions as a group of tangled threads. In the visualization, he must find the thread going from himself to his emotions and then he needs to cut all the other threads. Sometimes it helps to visualize all the emotions you are picking up on as different colored threads. Give colors to the threads based on where they are coming from. Those coming from the other person in the relationship could be red, those coming from other interested parties could be pink, and those coming from you could be yellow. Close your eyes and try to separate the yellow thread from the others, and hold onto it.

Yet another way of visualizing the situation is to use the idea of tunnel vision. A Pisces person can pretend they are wearing blinders like race horses to keep them from focusing on anything other than what is directly in front of them.

All of these exercises take practice in order to be able to do them at will, but they are worth the effort. The main thing is that you are trying to find a way that works for you that will help you separate your feelings from the feelings of others. So whether you use the colored thread method or the horse and blinders, or the visual picture of following a straight line between yourself and your emotions, the desired result is the same.

The second part of this exercise requires that you then lift yourself out of your emotions. If you have found your "yellow thread," hold onto it, then see yourself pulling it up to a higher level, above your head. That area above your head is the higher, more rational part of your nature, and you want to stay focused there.

If you are not a visual person, then saying mantras out loud is also a way to help you get out of an emotional morass. Words are very powerful, and so is suggestion, so that if we tell ourselves something often enough, we begin to believe it. If you know that you are going to be dealing with a difficult person, recite your mantra right before the meeting. This mantra needs to be prepared well ahead of time, and should be practiced sufficiently so that you can call upon it whenever you need it. You might write something like, "When my mother criticizes me, she is really criticizing herself," or you could use old standbys like "sticks and stones can break my bones...." Old standbys work just fine; you just need to make sure that you are truly listening to the words.

VIRGO

Virgo is the only earth sign we have not yet discussed. In the case of Virgo, they also bury their feelings when it comes to painfully difficult relationships, and their outward reaction is to look down upon the other person and walk away. They can be great snobs, and snobbery is many times a mask. A Virgo person is looking for perfection, both in themselves and in others. In their way of thinking, a perfect person would not hurt their feelings, and therefore if you are hurting their feelings, then you are imperfect and should be avoided.

The real truth of what they are feeling can only be reached by understanding that you have to penetrate the wall of rationality

IF THE RELATIONSHIP IS UNBEARABLE

they build. Their orthodox ruler is Mercury, and Mercury can give them the mental dexterity to play all kinds of mind games. They seek perfection and that is where the pain comes in, but they hide the pain through mental and verbal attributes. We earlier advised Cancers to focus on the mental plane in order to deal with emotional hurts. Virgos intuitively know how to do this.

So why don't we just leave them there, you ask? If they are already on the mental plane which protects them from pain, then shouldn't we applaud them? The reason we have to break through and go to the heart of the pain is because it needs to be handled correctly or else it will fester and manifest itself in an inappropriate way. That is the reason that we are asking all earth signs to break through their barriers and dig out the pain so that it can be dealt with properly. In the case of any of the feeling signs, the water signs, they know the pain is there, they feel it and know why they feel it. In the case of the earth signs, usually they don't acknowledge it is there and so do not allow themselves to feel it and know why they feel it. So our job is to make the Virgo person feel his pain, recognize its source and purpose, and then dispose of it. When you allow yourself to feel the pain, you then have the right to deal with it. Not before.

The opposite sign of Virgo, Pisces, provides a wonderful example for Virgos when it comes to feeling pain, for they feel everyone's. The Virgo person just needs a small bit of that compassion to come to the surface and he will be well on the way to recovery. Virgos are just as compassionate as Pisceans, they just don't show it. Their drive for perfection stands in the way, and so sometimes critical words rather than empathic words are the result.

An exercise for Virgos to use to learn how to overcome their drive for perfection is to visualize themselves as a small dewdrop in an ocean of dewdrops. Try to see yourself as connected to all the other dewdrops because you are all in the same sea. Up close, you notice that all of the dewdrops are different shapes

Astrology & Difficult Relationships: WHY ARE YOU IN MY LIFE?

and different sizes, but from a distance, they are all just dewdrops, no more, no less. Their differences are not imperfections, they are just differences that don't matter at all from a larger perspective.

If visualizations do not work for you, here are a few sample mantras. You might repeat to yourself, "I see the divinity in all men," or "My desire to serve is higher than my desire to criticize." The idea is to design a mantra that will allow you to bring your compassionate and accepting nature to the surface, and to eliminate the criticizing or perfectionist attitude that can stand in the way of relating.

CHAPTER FIVE

OBSTACLES TO RELATING

Just as there are emotional issues that can keep people from relating, there are also particular personality traits that can become obstacles to relating. The obstacles I am referring to are detrimental to relating because they can bring a sense of coldness and uncaring into the process. If one person does not care if the relationship works, then it is very difficult for things to get better. And if one person is perceived as cold, then again, it will be very difficult to improve the relationship.

The kinds of people who just don't seem to care if a relationship improves are usually people who are very mentally polarized or who are very self-contained, or very willful. Mentally polarized people can be so rational in their approach that they often do not see an emotional benefit to salvaging a relationship. Sensitivity and compassion do not enter into the picture. If they cannot rationally and logically make a case for saving a relationship, they will move on without giving it any more thought. People with very strong wills, on the other hand, will also walk away from a relationship simply because they are so self-contained and self-assured that they see no reason to relate to the other person.

The first type, the person who is entirely mentally focused, astrologically probably has a lot of the energy of any of the three mental signs, namely Gemini, Libra and Aquarius. The second type, the one who is so strong-willed that he is not afraid to cut his losses and move on, is usually someone with a lot of fire in his makeup, an Aries, Leo or Sagittarius type.

It is very clear how someone who is overly mental or overly willful can present an obstacle to relating, for they will not have any desire to see the relationship continue. So if you are in a difficult relationship with someone who just doesn't seem to care whether you resolve things or not, who is cold and aloof, or who is ready to move on, more than likely you are dealing with someone who has either of these two elements, air or fire, very strongly placed in their charts. The ways to bring them back into the relationship vary according to the sign involved, and so we will discuss ways to approach relating with fire and air sign individuals, beginning with the Aries and Libra polarity.

ARIES

Aries is the pioneer, the person who wants to be in the lead, to be the first to try something. Anyone with this energy strong in his or her chart will have a love of adventure, and so the new and unexplored is always calling. Therefore, if a strong Aries type is involved in a difficult relationship, they may just conclude that it isn't worth their time to fix it because there are more exciting and undiscovered relationships out there waiting for them.

If you want to relate better with these people, first take the time to really look at the relationship and see if it is one that should be continued. If it is one involving a parent, a child or a spouse, for instance, then of course you want to try to make it work. If it is an acquaintance, or a romantic partner, consider whether or not the relationship is worth repairing. If you conclude after the proper amount of soul searching that the relationship, though difficult, is worth saving, then read on. Otherwise, you may want to accept the fact that, like your Aries partner, there are better relationships waiting to be made and move on.

Aries people need you to give them a reason to stick

OBSTACLES TO RELATING

around. Guilt and criticism won't work with them. That is one of the things that they are probably running away from. No, what you need to do with an Aries type is to show that this relationship is exciting and interesting enough to be worth their time. At the same time, the Aries person needs to feel that he has the freedom to leave anytime he chooses. The key word here is freedom.

Most importantly, you have to show the Aries person that the purpose of the relationship is to do what he values most, that of initiating new ideas and leading the field in some way, and that the goal can be better reached with you as a partner than without you.

LIBRA

Librans are the mental ones in this combination, and so their perspective will be totally rational. They will have carefully weighed all the pros and cons and come up with a wise decision. If they leave the relationship, they will have many reasons why, logically, the relationship should end. Emotional pleadings will not work with them. They will only see logic.

Your best approach with a Libran, disgruntled enough with a relationship to simply call it quits, is to give them a long list of reasons why they should give more energy to the relationship. The list should be a complete as you can make it; get help if necessary. The Libran person will admire your thoroughness. Make sure that none of the reasons on the list are the least bit emotional or illogical. Venus rules Libra, and so while they do admire beauty and harmony, they do so in a very mental and logical way.

Librans want to relate, only they need a lot of information before doing so. Give them enough reasons to allow them to make a balanced decision regarding the value of the relationship, and they will re-commit to it.

Next we will look at the polarity of Gemini and Sagittarius.

Astrology & Difficult Relationships: WHY ARE YOU IN MY LIFE?

GEMINI

A Gemini, another of the mental signs, will again only respond to logic, but his reasons will be different from that of a Libra. Unlike the Libra who is concerned with gathering enough facts to make a correct decision, the Gemini gets bored easily and will not stick around unless he or she is mentally stimulated. Geminis can connect pieces of information very quickly and they are adept at seeing both sides of any issue. Once they have connected the pieces, they are ready to move on to the next problem.

If you are in a difficult relationship with someone who has a lot of Gemini energy, then you have to figure out how to hold their attention. If they have already tired of dealing with the relationship, probably because they no longer find it interesting, and have concluded logically that they should move on, then you will have to intelligently and persuasively argue that the relationship is worth continuing. Your argument must not only be intelligent and persuasive, it must be entertaining as well and not be too tedious. Geminis like a light touch, and are bored by a lot of detail or excess emotionalism. Don't ever appear desperate to them, for they will interpret this as too much of an emotional arena for them to be involved in. Geminis love mental exercises. Make your argument mental and interesting and they will stick around.

SAGITTARIUS

This is the fire sign opposite the sign Gemini, and so it is related to that sign in many ways. But while a person with a lot of Gemini energy in their makeup is apt to lose attention quickly, a Sagittarian will stay focused and will pursue his goal with a single pointed vigor. They will not waver, and they will be out front, leading you to their desired end. So in a relationship with a Sagittarius person, if your goal is not in line with theirs, expect there to be major difficulties.

Once you understand their motivation, it is easy to see why the Sagittarius person would simply walk away from a difficult relationship if he feels that the relationship is going in a direction different from the direction in which he is headed. The glyph for Sagittarius is an arrow and it illustrates this concept clearly, for they know exactly where they are going. While the person on the other end may be totally devastated because the Sagittarian walked away, the Sagittarian person did it with absolutely no malice; he simply has to follow his own lead. A Sagittarian person would probably disagree that their innate desire to follow their own lead would in any way pose an obstacle to relating; they believe in truth and will follow their truth wherever it leads.

Trouble is, their truth may not be your truth, and so the difficulty is in getting them to come back and take a look at your truth and consider a change in direction, or at least a compromise. All of the fire signs enjoy a competition, and sometimes if you can make them see that the prize at the end, a harmonious relationship, is worth fighting for, they will try again to relate. The best way to turn around a Sagittarian is to appeal to his love of the truth. All of the fire signs have a strong mental component due to the fact that they are all on the polarity of air and fire. So the truthful approach to your Sagittarian should definitely have a mental and not an emotional focus. As with all the fire signs, Sagittarian types love their freedom, so do not try to use any kind of controlling methods or guilt trips to force them to return to the relationship. Simply state the truth, your truth, in an intelligent and honest way.

Finally, we will look at the Leo/Aquarius polarity in their role as potential obstacles to relating.

Astrology & Difficult Relationships: WHY ARE YOU IN MY LIFE?

LEO

We all know that people with a lot of Leo in their astrological make-ups can be prone to self-centeredness. This is not all bad, in that the function of Leo energy is to help us develop a strong sense of who we are. But when this is carried to the extreme, it can result in some very selfish, authoritarian people. In relationships, self-centeredness and selfishness are by definition harmful to the process of relating, for in relationships, we are asked to look beyond ourselves and consider the thoughts and feelings of the other person. It is quite easy to see, then, how a Leo person who is extremely self-centered, would not be bothered with a relationship if it were not going the way he wanted, or if it were not in some way embellishing his personal image.

If you are involved in a relationship with a Leo person, and that person has chosen to walk away from the relationship, it is probably because he cannot see how it would benefit him to stay. Your job, then, is to show the Leo person how the relationship will benefit him, and at the same time, move the relationship forward. The Leo has detached himself from the relationship, which he views as his right; you must appeal to his largesse and show him how the greater good is served if he stays attached.

Approaching the Leo head on will usually result in your losing the fight. Leos are superior warriors and in a frontal attack, you will most likely be crushed. Remember that they are related to the lion, the king of the jungle. A lion must be approached strategically. Leo is a fire sign and so they know how to handle fire; you must get out of that element to have any chance of winning. The best way to approach them is to appeal to their well-known lion heart. They are famous for their generosity. Leos are also well known for their desire to have a good time. Take the drudgery out of the relationship and see to it that it is enjoyable for both of you. Like other fire signs, Leos are very competitive,

OBSTACLES TO RELATING

so you may want to bring in an element of competition to get their attention. The idea of a prize worth competing for can take the form of the fun that can be had in the relationship if the differences are worked out.

Once your foot is in the door, you have to appeal to their higher natures and to their humanitarian side. All Leos are protective of those weaker than themselves, and so appeal to that leonine trait. You want the Leo person to see that by being generous in the relationship, both of you will benefit.

AQUARIUS

Aquarian energy is full of movement, hence the wavy lines in the glyph of this sign. An Aquarian is quite bright, and able to see clearly into the future. They can see things before you can even sense them, due to their tie to Uranus, the planet that rules the new and revolutionary. So they will get rid of anything they consider old, worn-out, and in need of replacement without a second thought. This applies to everything in their lives, including relationships.

If you are in a difficult relationship with an Aquarius type and he has determined that the relationship is outmoded and walks away, then you are going to have to develop a new, more appropriate and revolutionary way of relating to this person. Otherwise, don't expect to see him again. While Geminis want variety, and Librans want reasons, an Aquarian wants a new and better way of relating. So if you want a typical mother-daughter relationship, the kind of relationship where you go shopping every weekend, and she calls you on the phone all the time, you may have to give up that idea if you want to maintain a relationship with an Aquarian daughter. If your spouse is Aquarian born, you may have to live with the idea of having a totally non-conventional marriage; you may live in separate homes and only see each other a few times per year. But just because the structure of the relationship is

Astrology & Difficult Relationships: WHY ARE YOU IN MY LIFE?

unconventional does not mean that the relationship cannot be a solid one. The main point to remember here is that you are striving to devise a way of relating that works for the two of you.

While you are devising your updated method of relating, remember that the Aquarian person, like the other air signs, views life in a rational and unemotional way, so your approach must not only be original, but it must also be detached.

So in dealing with difficult air or fire people, if you can turn excess air or fire into positives, then the relationships will gain an added dimension. Relationships become more alive when fire is added, and they will become more illumined when fresh air blows through.

CHAPTER SIX

WILL THE RELATIONSHIP IMPROVE?

If you have been struggling in a difficult relationship for some time, you may feel as if it is never going to get any better. Sometimes, though, we lose hope when there is no reason to do so. Sometimes, we simply need to try another tactic or adopt a new approach. We might be more willing to try something different if we knew that the relationship held out some hope of success. How, then, do we determine if there is any reason to feel hope?

The way we determine astrologically if there really is hope for a particular relationship is to look for any trines and sextiles between the two charts. Trines and sextiles represent the possibility of reconciliation. The trines are the more hopeful of the two aspects, but sextiles present much opportunity. You can relate to that particular person quite easily in the area of your life affected by a trine or sextile. Even if all other areas of life are difficult, that one area represented by the trine or sextile will be neutral territory. The secret is to learn how to use the areas of life involving the trines or sextiles as a springboard into the area that is troubling. Or to put it another way, you have to figure out how to use that one area of agreement to fix the areas that are malfunctioning. A man who cannot talk to his father about anything except sports, for instance, must learn how to parlay that into a door that opens communication in all areas. A woman who fights with her mother about everything except cooking must figure out how they can turn that enjoyable hobby into a segue for peace.

Sometimes the areas where we can easily relate are hidden to us, and that is where astrology can help. Maybe you don't know that your cousin, whom you dislike, has his Pluto trining your Sun. This is a huge opening for you to "shine a light" on his potential for power and affect a major transformation in his life. You haven't tried to do anything to help him, and yet your astrology shows that you can. Or suppose that your mother-in-law has been giving you a hard time. You discover that her Uranus sextiles your Mercury, therefore giving you the opportunity to reach some sort of new and revolutionary way of dealing with your problems through discussion and communication, but you have not even considered discussing the issues with her because of your anger.

If a trine or sextile exists, then there is hope. Trines occur between planets that are 120 degrees apart (with an orb of 7 degrees) so they normally occur between signs of the same quadriplicity, i.e., between two fire signs, two earth signs, two air signs or two water signs. Trines between two fire signs will be full of fire and passion, and the two people will move forward in a fiery and self-confident way. Trines between two earth signs will have a practicality and a common sense approach to the relationship. Trines between two air signs indicate a mental polarization, and thus the parties will approach situations in a rational and intelligent way. Trines between two water signs will have an ease in emotional relating, for they will both understand how compassion, empathy and sensitivity help move any relationship along.

There is also what is known as an out-of-sign trine. For instance, you might have a planet at 29 degrees of Taurus and your difficult mother-in-law has a planet at 1 degree of Libra. This is an out-of-sign trine, but a trine nonetheless. It is not between two signs of the same quadraplicity, i.e., air and air, or water and water, but between an air sign and a water sign. To analyze the meaning of an out-of-sign trine, you must look at the meanings of the different quadraplicities and how they would interact.

WILL THE RELATIONSHIP IMPROVE?

Sextiles occur between planets that are 60 degrees apart, thus they will normally occur between air and fire signs, and between water and earth signs. Sextiles between air and fire signs mean that an intelligent approach will be used along with the passion of the fire signs, so the combination can keep the fire sign person from moving too fast and making mistakes, and the air sign gets pushed out of its intellectual tower into true activity in the real world. The result is that much is accomplished in an intelligent way. Sextiles between water and earth signs afford the opportunity to unite the practicality of the earth sign along with the sensitivity of the water sign, the result being a compassionate manifesting of structures upon the physical plane.

Again, you can have sextiles that are out-of-sign, and you will have to spend a little more time to properly interpret them, noting the relationship of the quadraplicities of the signs involved.

The meaning of these trines and sextiles in relationships and the ways they can be used as springboards into other areas of the relationship are discussed below by angle, planet and sign.

ASCENDANT

If someone has a planet that trines or sextiles your Ascendant, you should be extremely hopeful for the relationship, for this indicates that the other person can be beneficial to your soul purpose. You two can find a way to relate. The Ascendant is what we are striving to become, and this person can help you in that quest. This person supports you in some way, and it is up to you to figure out how they can help you to achieve your soul purpose and then allow them to do it.

DESCENDANT

A trine or sextile to your Descendant is an indication of a true partner. This person brings to the relationship those qualities that you are lacking, so the two of you together form a completed whole and are able to accomplish much more than either of you could alone. Use this person's qualities to help you to round out your own. More importantly, use this true partner to work through the problems areas, knowing that he is as dedicated to the partnership as you are.

NADIR

The Nadir has to do with your emotional and psychological foundation, and so a trine or sextile to this angle will add to your emotional stability. This person may have something to offer that could positively change your entire emotional or psychological outlook on life, so you should pay close attention to what they are offering. Or, the person may have a similar background as yours and thus may be totally in line with your views and emotional responses. And because you can feel comfortable emotionally with this person, you can use this as a springboard to be open and honest in your feelings and thus begin to heal the other areas of your relationship.

MIDHEAVEN

Trines and sextiles to your Midheaven indicate that this person is going to be very helpful and beneficial to your career or profession. If you are unclear as to what you should be doing with your life, they can be of assistance in some way. Use your career as an excuse to tackle the other areas in your life where you are having problems with this person. Knowing that they are going to be beneficial to your standing in the world should allow you to trust them in other areas of your life.

WILL THE RELATIONSHIP IMPROVE?

VERTEX

A trine or sextile to your vertex indicates that this particular relationship is one that is fated and that you are definitely supposed to deal with in this lifetime. Knowing that it is a fated relationship should give you confidence that by addressing the problems of the relationship, you are doing the right thing and heading in the right direction. Follow it through and you, along with the other person, will reach that point of liberation, the anti-vertex. The trine or sextile is an indication that everything is destined to work out in a good way.

ANTI-VERTEX

A trine or sextile from another person to your anti-vertex suggests a past life connection, or the possibility of a potent lesson which has been learned together. This is a position of joy and freedom, and so the two of you are in a unique position to conquer whatever it is that needs conquering in this lifetime, because you have already been through an important life experience together. This trine or sextile indicates that you need not be afraid to tackle a difficult relationship because you have shown that you have the necessary courage to handle anything that may arise.

SUN

A trine or sextile from another person's chart to your Sun is very positive for it indicates that the person is supportive of your creativity and the way you express yourself. In other words, you can be totally at ease with this person. You should feel very comfortable, then, in investigating the other troublesome areas because you know that the person is on your side.

Astrology & Difficult Relationships: WHY ARE YOU IN MY LIFE?

MOON

The Moon represents your past and your emotional base, so anyone having a planet trining or sextiling your Moon either has a past life connection to you or they are in tune with you emotionally or psychologically. They understand how you feel and react to things. Therefore, you can feel free to discuss painful and troublesome issues with them for they will be able to understand your point of view.

MERCURY

A trine or sextile to your Mercury from the other person's chart is an indication that you have an open channel of communication, and as we all know, communication is extremely important in relationships. So whatever the issue is that is dividing you, the two of you should be able to talk it out intelligently. As the Mercury person, you are in a particularly strong position to be able to see both sides of the issue and therefore to be able to come up with intelligent and thoughtful ways for bridging the gap.

VENUS

A trine or sextile to the Venus of either party in an otherwise difficult relationship indicates that the way out of the controversy is through loving understanding. The Venus person has a most powerful energy that she can bring to the table, and if used correctly, the other person will feel that love and the relationship will be lifted. If the Venus trine or sextile works correctly, the two people should be able to heal their relationship simply because they can look past the lower personality issues and see the higher spiritual possibilities.

WILL THE RELATIONSHIP IMPROVE?

MARS

If your Mars is trined or sextiled by a planet in another person's chart, then you are the catalyst for positive energy, and this energy can be used to take the relationship where it is supposed to go. You can together use this energy to attack the issues that are dividing you, to turn the relationship around so that it is headed in the right direction, and then revitalize it. While Mars can make some horrible things happen if you are fighting, if you both commit to using the energy together in a positive way, it can turn both of you into warriors dedicated to achieving your combined goal.

JUPITER

Jupiter all by itself is wonderful, and so if you have a Jupiter trine or sextile in your relationship, there is absolutely no reason why the two of you cannot resolve the issues that are dividing you, for Jupiter will provide the optimism and sense of camaraderie necessary for any relationship to grow. Jupiter will expand the feelings of goodwill brought by the other person's planet, and so combined, the two of you will be inspired to make sure that things work out. This enthusiasm and inspiration are the tools that you will use to overcome all obstacles in your relationship.

SATURN

A Saturn trine or sextile in relationships will provide that sense of commitment and responsibility necessary to make sure that both of you stay the course. Where Saturn is involved, you will both feel obligated to do the necessary work to clear up the problems. Saturn trines and sextiles can also be indicative of a karmic past, or at least of some sort of connection that is deeper than meets the eye. The bottom line is that the positive energy of Saturn is available for use by the partnership. This energy can be used to bring a mature, responsible and disciplined attitude to the situation, aiding in the development of the necessary right actions to take the relationship to a higher level.

URANUS

A trine or sextile involving Uranus will indicate that the relationship is forward looking. It may be a stormy relationship, one constantly changing, but changing for the better. Uranus is the planet of originality. It is also the planet of brotherhood, and so a trine or sextile to Uranus indicates that the relationship has a universal, loving quality about it. You respect each other as human beings, and therefore, will find an original and ingenious way to relate, a way that satisfies the needs of both parties.

NEPTUNE

Neptune is the planet of idealism, and so, trines and sextiles from Neptune will allow the partnership to visualize the best that it can be. If the two persons can hold onto this vision, then their reactions will always be of the highest level and their motivations will always be pure. No matter what area of life in which Neptune starts this visualization process, it should not be too difficult to enlarge the vision to include the problem areas of the relationship as well.

PLUTO

Trines and sextiles involving Pluto will have a positive transformative effect on the partnership. Pluto will also bring power and intensity to the area of life it highlights. This power and intensity can be used to tackle the difficult areas of the relationship and to transform them into what they should really be. Use the Pluto energy to rid the relationship of all of the poisonous thoughts, ideas, words, etc. that are keeping you from properly relating.

CHIRON

If a Chiron trine or sextile is involved in a relationship, then resolving the issues will bring healing, and so that should be an impetus to get going and try to figure out a way to relate. Try to bring old wounds to the surface and work your way through them together. Chiron, because of its relationship to Sagittarius, will also give you an indication of the direction in which you need to take the relationship so that this healing process can begin.

JUNO

Trines and sextiles to Juno are an indication that this can be a truly committed partnership. Juno's presence in any relationship is always an indication of hope, because this asteroid is all about relating. Juno in mythology is the goddess of marriage, and so the two of you can form a "marriage" of sorts. This idea can be translated to all areas of life, and like any good marriage, you can learn how to compromise so that both sides are melded into one functioning unit.

CERES

Trines or sextiles involving Ceres are an indication that the partnership has the ability to nurture itself and thus make the relationship better. Ceres brings the image of nourishing or feeding the area of life it is concerned with, so use this image to nourish and feed the problem areas in the relationship, so that it can grow and develop properly and finally mature into something

Astrology & Difficult Relationships: WHY ARE YOU IN MY LIFE?

beautiful.

VESTA

Vesta implies sacrifice and dedication, a dedication or sacrifice to a person, a cause, a belief, etc. Trines and sextiles from Vesta, then, indicate that the possibility exists for a total sacrifice and dedication to the beliefs and goals of the partnership. This kind of total dedication can be used to bring the partnership to a totally new level, for it indicates that the parties in the partnership can be counted on to make the necessary sacrifices to ensure its success.

PALLAS ATHENE

Trines and sextiles involving Pallas Athene indicate the ability to shrewdly and analytically address partnership issues. Pallas Athene in mythology was a military strategist and would be consulted by the various gods before going into battle. As superb strategists, the members of the partnership come up with a brilliant strategy for fixing the broken parts of their relationship.

Next, we will address trines based upon the quadriplicities, i.e., fire sign trines, air sign trines, earth sign trines, and water sign trines. You are left to interpolate the meanings of out-of-sign trines on your own.

ARIES/LEO

An Aries/Leo trine will mean that the two of you are bringing powerful energies and leadership abilities to the area of life in which the trine is located. You two can shake up the world, for you are full of the passion of life. The Aries energy will push you forward and the Leo energy will allow you to administer the

WILL THE RELATIONSHIP IMPROVE?

energies in an executive way. The relationship will be a powerhouse, and this much positive energy can be easily transferred to the other areas of life that are troublesome. This energy can be used to dispel the problem areas and get the partnership headed in a better direction.

ARIES/SAGITTARIUS

Aries wants to go forward, and Sagittarius is always shooting out his arrows to follow them, so the combination works well in pursuing a similar goal. If the two of you can sense where the relationship is destined to go, and this should be very easy for the Sagittarius person, then there will be an almost fearlessness in going there. With this combination, whether the goal is to overcome fears, raise levels of consciousness, or eliminate prejudices, etc., it can be accomplished simply because of the innate vision and courage brought to bear by this trine.

LEO/SAGITTARIUS

Leo has strong executive skills, and Sagittarius is visionary and driven towards his goal, so the two energies together will lead the relationship toward its desired destination in a well-managed and well-executed way. The Leo energy will help temper the Sagittarian tendency to sometimes enthusiastically overreach the goal or to behave in a clownish manner, by seeing to it that things are done in a grand and dignified way. The Sagittarian person provides the single-mindedness and direction, keeping the relationship from getting off track.

TAURUS/VIRGO

The Taurus person will bring the strong desire to fix things, and Virgo will bring the detail and patience to do it right.

Astrology & Difficult Relationships: WHY ARE YOU IN MY LIFE?

The symbol of Taurus, the bull, reminds us of their trait of being slow to action, but once they start moving, they are quite powerful. This characteristic works well with the Virgo energy, for the Virgo needs time to plan carefully. So the trine between these two is a lovely dance of gradually intensifying, sensual, discriminative and precise action. To watch a Taurean and Virgoan build something together is quite beautiful. But more importantly, what they build will be solid, strong, and therefore lasting. These signs both work well in the material world; their only problem is going to be that they make sure that what they patiently build together is motivated by the highest of desires, for they will surely build whatever it is they set out to do together.

TAURUS/CAPRICORN

Capricorn energy works through mastery of self-determination and a steely ambition; Taurus energy succeeds in the world through perseverance and a steady approach. The two energies together bring a mindset that is totally focused on success. The two animal images of these signs, the bull and the goat, sum this up quite nicely. Taurus uses its warmth and appreciation of beauty to soften the massive ambition that is Capricorn by slowing it down and forcing it to "smell the roses" from time to time, and the Capricorn person uses its strategic planning abilities and broad perspective to lead them with a steady hand to the "mountaintop" or goal, of the relationship.

VIRGO/CAPRICORN

The precision of Virgo works very well with the strategic abilities of the Capricorn. The Capricorn outlines in bold strokes the safest and surest way to fulfill the purpose of the relationship, and the Virgo person then takes over and painstakingly fills in all the details. The person bringing the Capricorn energy will take the lead, and the Virgo person will work quietly behind the scenes, in a more supportive role. The two, though, will be committed to the same goal, and will mutually respect each other's talents and contributions to its achievement. This is an excellent working combination.

GEMINI/LIBRA

The Gemini individual brings to this trine the ability to look at all sides of the situation, and the Libra individual brings the ability to make the correct choice after weighing all the information. This is a rational approach to relating, one that removes all emotion and other extraneous factors from the decision—making process. This is quite helpful, for it allows the parties to be quite clear and precise in making their choices and that helps to insure that the proper choice is made. Clear, enlightened thinking leads to intuition, and intuition, i.e., doing what you know is right, is always the best way to proceed in any relationship, for it ensures that the best choice will prevail.

GEMINI/AQUARIUS

Again, we have the Gemini ability to clearly see all sides of an issue, and be able to articulate those sides to the other person. The Aquarian person adds to this their innate understanding of the connection of all humans and their innate desire to relate. The Gemini says here are all the reasons that things aren't working, and the Aquarian says I want to make things work at all costs, and between them, using again a rational, mental approach, they craft a workable solution. Gemini is open to all possibilities, and the Aquarian person offers the unique and unusual solution. They will find a way to relate, albeit it unusual, but it will work for them and their relationship.

Astrology & Difficult Relationships: WHY ARE YOU IN MY LIFE?

LIBRA/AQUARIUS

The Libra person wants a lot of information so that he can weigh it all before he makes up his mind. The Aquarius person wants to do things in the most innovative and creative way. The two of these energies together create a unique, thoughtful solution to their relating problems. Librans want harmonious relationships, and Aquarius energy wants to make everyone their friend, therefore there is a tremendous desire in this combination to relate no matter what the problem. Such commitment to overcoming relationship problems guarantees success in doing so.

CANCER/SCORPIO

This combination brings an emotional and passionate quality to the relationship. The Cancer person is very sensitive to the needs of others, and the Scorpio person feels very deeply, and the result is that the two together will be able to form a relationship and a way of relating that is sensitive to the feelings and needs of each other. The sensitive Cancer person will be able to step into the shoes of the other person, thereby increasing understanding, and the passionate feeling Scorpio person will be able to understand with depth the feelings of the Cancer person. Sensitivity and depth of feeling, when properly placed, allow for an open discussion where no one gets hurt and both viewpoints are understood.

CANCER/PISCES

When the two most sensitive signs of the zodiac get together, a higher level of intuition and understanding will prevail. They understand each other's needs without talking, for they can touch each other's feelings. As a result, problems in a relationship will be dealt with intuitively, in a manner that is soft, loving and caring. The Cancer energy will provide the nurturing "home" for the discussions to take place, and the Pisces energy will provide the compassionate understanding.

SCORPIO/PISCES

Scorpio energy is intense, and Pisces energy is loving and compassionate. Therefore, the two energies together can create an intensely loving and compassionate relationship. Pisces is the last sign of the zodiac, thus it encompasses the traits of all the signs, and Scorpio is the sign that can penetrate into the depths of any situation, so together you have an all encompassing, deep and wide understanding of the problems of the relationship. The Scorpio person will get to the root of the matter and bring to the surface all the problems, and the Pisces person will help to dissolve the problems in a loving and understanding way.

Finally, we will look at the sextiles based on modality, that is, fire/air and earth/water.

ARIES/GEMINI

This combination represents the opportunity, if used, to bring a passionate and at the same time, rational approach to the underlying issues of the relationship. The passion or fire of the Aries person can be used in an intelligent way, so that the energy is not dissipated. Additionally, the Aries person can kick the Gemini person out of its intellectual ivory tower and force it to take action in the world rather than just theorizing all the time. Good theories combined with courageous action can lead to major progress.

Astrology & Difficult Relationships: WHY ARE YOU IN MY LIFE?

ARIES/AQUARIUS

The Aquarius person will bring the desire to improve the relationship in new and innovative ways, and the Aries person will provide the impetus to put the new relating model into practice, so the opportunity exists here to move the relationship from a bad place to a much better place. The Aries energy responds well to the Aquarian new ideas for Aries always wants to be in the forefront, and the Aquarius energy adds excitement to the venture, so the opportunity exists to totally revamp the relationship.

LEO/GEMINI

Another fire/air combination, this one takes intellectualism and combines it with administrative skill, the result being an intelligent moving forward. The Leo person will not want to do the theorizing; that will be left up to the one bringing the Gemini energy. But once the plan is devised, the Leo will be a master at implementing it in broad strokes. The Gemini person has great ideas, and the Leo person has great leadership abilities and the two together build creative and dynamic unions.

LEO/LIBRA

The person with the Leo energy wants to have fun and enjoy life and the relationship, and the person with the Libra energy wants harmony and peace in the relationship. The two have the opportunity to work well to improve their relationship by crafting a fun and harmonious setting in which to address all of their problems. This is a sextile of atmosphere; the atmosphere that they will create is conducive to working together to heal all their relationship ills.

WILL THE RELATIONSHIP IMPROVE?

SAGITTARIUS/LIBRA

The Sagittarian person is going to want to move forward in the relationship; the Libra person will need time to weigh all the factors and make sure he has made the correct decision before he moves. The two will temper each other, for the Sagittarian will have to wait and thus not make as many false moves; the Libran will be lulled from the comfort of procrastination. The two together bring a balanced approach to the relationship and to the issues that need to be worked on.

SAGITTARIUS/AQUARIUS

The Sagittarian person is very goal oriented; the Aquarian is future minded. The two together will fashion a way to relate that is constantly moving towards their goal. Both bring vision, but of a different kind. The Sagittarian's vision is intuitional; the Aquarian's vision is tied to his genius. The two together can form a combined vision that is exciting enough and revolutionary enough for both parties to stay interested long enough to reach their relationship goal.

TAURUS/CANCER

Taurus, when relating is very down to earth; Cancer is very sensitive. The Taurus person wants to feel comfortable in the relationship; the Cancer person wants to show and receive love. Therefore, this can be a very comfortable combination as the Taurus person will find down to earth, sensible ways of relating, and the Cancer person will see to it that the warm and cozy feeling pervades the relationship as well. The two of them instinctively understand the harm that discord and disharmony can do.

Astrology & Difficult Relationships: WHY ARE YOU IN MY LIFE?

TAURUS/PISCES

The Taurus is able to show his gentle side with Pisces, for the Taurean appreciates the sensitivity of the Pisces individual. The Pisces person brings the compassion and understanding from higher realms, and the Taurus person helps to ground the Pisces person, due to their very stable and earthy nature. Within a framework of loving understanding and peace, the two can easily resolve their issues and they can put the relationship on the right track.

VIRGO/CANCER

Virgo has an eye for detail, and Cancer has a good feel for the relationship. The Cancer can intuitively sense what needs to be fixed, and the Virgo can devise a systematic and detailed plan to carry out the work. The Cancer relates to the Virgo through feeling, and gets a sense of how to make the relationship work, while the Virgo takes a more mental approach to the task. The result is that the relationship is very finely tuned due to the extreme sensitivity of the Cancer and the deft craftsmanship of the Virgo.

VIRGO/SCORPIO

The Virgo person can meticulously put plans into action, making sure no detail is overlooked. The Scorpio person can penetrate to the depths of a situation in order to understand it, and rid it of any hindrances to correct operations. The two together will work as analytical detectives to get to the bottom of their particular relating problem, and then with deftness and exactitude, will eliminate all of the offending issues, and painstakingly build a better, more solid and more perfect union.

WILL THE RELATIONSHIP IMPROVE?

CAPRICORN/SCORPIO

The Capricorn person will bring the perspective and the skills to achieve a correctly defined goal. The Scorpio person has the ability to penetrate to the depths to identify the hidden issues that have been hindering correct relating. The two together are a powerful combination, for once the Scorpio has identified and eliminated the harmful underlying issues, the success of the relationship is assured, for the Capricorn person will see to it that they reach the highest that is possible in their relationship.

CAPRICORN/PISCES

A sextile between Capricorn and Pisces brings in all the beautiful compassion and understanding of the Pisces individual along with the common sense of the Capricorn. The result is that the two people can bring down from above luminous qualities and make them materialize in the real world. This is an excellent combination for making idealistic attitudes a reality. This kind of idealism plus pragmatism can make any relationship better.

CHAPTER SEVEN

WALKING IN ANOTHER'S SHOES

We have all heard many times that we should not judge another person until we have walked a mile in their shoes. I am sure that all of us would agree that if we could step into another person's shoes and see the world from his or her perspective, that we would be able to tremendously improve our relationships because our perspective would be so much broader.

The idea of seeing life from another's perspective is a great one, but not so easy to do in real life. Luckily for us as students of astrology, we are given a tool that will allow us to easily see the other person's perspective, if we choose to. How do we walk in another person's shoes astrologically? **By looking at the squares and oppositions in our relationships.**

Squares and oppositions are an indication of disharmony. They point out to us the places where we are "in opposition" to the other persons' views, and where we are "square" against them. For instance, if your Sun squares someone else's Sun, there are obstacles related to self-expression that have to be eliminated before the relationship can proceed smoothly. The house in which the square occurs indicates the area of life where these obstacles occur. If your Sun falls in his third house, for instance, he will perceive that the obstacle relates to communication. If his Sun falls in your sixth house, you will perceive the obstacle as relating to work, health or service. The signs involved will flavor the nature of these obstacles.

Astrology, therefore, makes us walk in the other person's shoes by creating these obstacles or oppositions. The only way that the obstacles or oppositions can be eliminated is to adjust your position based upon his. In an opposition, this causes compromise. With squares, there is a removal of something in your point of view or attitude or behavior that is obstructing positive relating. If we want to clear the obstacles and oppositions in our relationships, we must take the other person's values into consideration. We must walk in their shoes.

In order to walk in someone else's shoes astrologically, you need to sit down and make a list of the characteristics of the sign or planet of the other person involved in the opposition or square. This may be difficult, especially in the case of the square, for the characteristics may be totally foreign to you. In the case of oppositions, it is a little easier, for since you are on the same axis, just at opposite ends, you may have some of the character traits in the negative, or at least you may be aware of them. A Gemini opposing a Sagittarian might have on the list things like honesty, moral compass, single mindedness, things a Gemini may have considered at one time and then moved on to other more interesting things. But, a Gemini squaring a Virgo might list things like neatness, discrimination, fastidiousness, or attention to detail, traits that most Geminis would not ordinarily consider.

A Leo opposing an Aquarius might list things like group involvement, friendships, humanitarian efforts, putting others first, all things that a Leo may have considered whenever they stepped outside their box. But a Leo squaring a Scorpio might list Scorpionic qualities such as penetrating intellect, deep emotions, long memory, all qualities that are not necessarily easy for a Leo person to understand.

Squares and oppositions can be overcome if we intelligently and diligently seek to ascertain what must be changed and then set out with positive intent to do it. With a square, you must look inside yourself only, with an opposition, you must figure out where you need to compromise. The square is therefore more difficult to overcome than the opposition, but well worth the effort. The energies involved in a square can be transformed into that of the trine, meaning that if the obstacle is removed, then the energies between the two planets can flow smoothly. A similar analogy can be made with the opposition. If the two planets that are in opposition can be made to meet in the middle, then the energy of the two planets becomes like the conjunction, and we all know that the conjunction is the most powerful of the aspects.

Now we are ready to take a look at the general meaning of squares and oppositions between planets and signs. Of course, you will have to take into consideration the houses involved to understand the area of life in which the aspect applies. The meanings of the houses were discussed back in Chapter Two. But the basic meaning of the square or opposition is the most important here, and that is why we are looking at each planet individually, plus the angles.

ASCENDANT

The Ascendant represents your true self, your soul, and your soul's potential. It is how you represent yourself to the world, and so anytime that someone has a planet that squares or opposes the Ascendant of another person, there is a major perspective problem that needs to be addressed. If you have a planet squaring or opposing someone's Ascendant, then you are at odds with where they need to go in their life. You may be standing in the way of their spiritual progress, or you may be creating problems for them because you refuse to compromise or you may be at odds with their beliefs.

The direction in which a person is to travel in this lifetime is very important to their spiritual growth, therefore, anything that you can do to assist them would not only be a great benefit to them, but it would also allow you to earn brownie points for aiding someone else along life's highway. Everyone benefits.

If your Sun, for instance, squares the Ascendant of a person whom you consider to be difficult, ask yourself if you are perhaps highlighting their faults for the wrong reasons. Maybe you should not be highlighting their faults at all. Maybe you should be helping them to highlight their skills, their best character traits, or their dreams. By so doing, you may help them make their dream a reality. (NOTE: If you have a planet that squares the Ascendant of someone, it also squares their Descendant, so pay close attention to the next section as well.)

Let's take another example. If your Saturn is opposing someone else's Ascendant, then both of you need to compromise a little. Since you are only responsible for your actions, you need only address how your Saturn can be toned down a bit in relation to this person so that the two of you can better relate. Perhaps you are trying to restrict their actions too much. Or maybe you are always prophesizing gloom and doom every time they have an idea. If you could be a little less restrictive and a little less gloomy, perhaps the structure and foundation that you offer as the Saturn person would be welcomed.

DESCENDANT

The Descendant is the opposite of the Ascendant or soul. It is the other self. If someone's Descendant is squared by a planet or angle in another person's chart, you may be responding to a particular trait in the other person that is buried in you that needs to be overcome. Or, you may be responding negatively to the person because he or she represents all the traits that you are lacking. If the latter is the case, then it will take you some time to understand the other person, because they are doing things in the exact opposite way in which you would do them.

Astrology & Difficult Relationships: WHY ARE YOU IN MY LIFE?

For instance, if someone's Mercury is squaring your Descendant, you probably have a hard time communicating with them; you don't understand each other, at least in the area of relationships. You think he talks too much, or too little, or he says the wrong thing at the wrong time. A walk in their shoes would show you the need to be a little bit more flexible in how you communicate and in how you interpret his words and ideas.

If your Jupiter opposes someone's Descendant, the other person may feel that you are overly optimistic, and you feel that the other person is a party pooper where your efforts at relating are concerned. You may need to tone down your spirits a bit, so as to make the other person more comfortable.

NADIR

The Nadir is the foundation of your life, and so anyone with planets squaring or opposing your Nadir is going to make you truly uncomfortable. We do not easily change our base or our emotional response apparatus. If you are the one whose Nadir is being squared or opposed, when you are around the other person you probably feel that your personal security is being threatened.

Mars, for instance, squaring your Nadir, would make you put up a wall of defense. From your perspective, the other person is just too aggressive. The only way to overcome this obstacle is to figure out what it is that makes the Mars person see red when they are around you. Maybe you are a bit too set in your ways and refuse to try anything new or to react in a way that is outside of your boundaries. On the other side of the coin, the Mars person needs to understand that you as the Nadir person see him as being overly aggressive and that he needs to tone down his behavior.

With the opposition, the adjustment to be made by each party won't be quite as drastic as will be required for the square. For instance, if someone's Pluto were opposing your Nadir, a meeting in the middle would require you both to give a little; you could be a little more flexible about security issues and take a chance now and then. The Pluto person could be a little less domineering and not try to control or mastermind everything.

MIDHEAVEN

Since the Midheaven represents one's calling in the world, or one's dharma, obstacles and oppositions can be very stressful. If someone has a planet squaring your Midheaven, there is an obstacle that is keeping you from pursuing your calling. If Mercury is the squaring planet, for instance, removing the obstacle may require that you eliminate the mental block you have to communication with this person. If Uranus is the squaring planet, you can remove the obstacle by allowing yourself to become more flexible, or to stop being afraid of change.

Oppositions to the Midheaven require compromises such as allowing the other person more input or control if Pluto is the opposing planet, showing more concern and consideration for the other person if Neptune is the opposing planet, or allowing the other person to have a greater input of thoughts and ideas if Mercury is the opposing planet.

Removing your fixed ideas in the case of the square, or allowing compromise and flexibility in the case of the opposition will allow your career to progress and blossom in a way that is not possible without the aid of the other person.

VERTEX

Representing fate or destiny, squares to the Vertex would mean that removing or overcoming the obstacle is important in realizing that destiny. That should give you extra incentive to really work on identifying the obstacle and developing ways to remove it. We wouldn't want to have anything standing in the way of our destiny. The same thing is true with the opposition to a lesser degree. The sooner we can identify the changes or adjustments, however slight, that need to be made for good relating, the sooner we will be able to go on the larger reward, that of fulfilling our destiny.

Therefore, if your Vertex squares someone's Pluto, for instance, lessen your grip on them. They perceive you as desiring to control them, and so they are not able to give you the help they could in pursuing your life goal. If your Vertex opposes their Mercury, then communication issues or irrational thinking on your part may be dooming the relationship. Therefore, you need to work on talking to them in a way they will view as rational and sane, then they will be able to better help you in pursuit of your destiny.

ANTI-VERTEX

Referred to sometimes as the point of freedom, it is that place where, having lived up to your destiny, or accepted your fate, you are now free to pursue your true calling, to discover your true self, and to live your true and honest life. If there is a square or opposition from someone in a difficult relationship, then they are telling you that something you are doing is not quite right if you are to live your true life, and it is more pronounced with the square.

If, for example, their Mars squares your Vertex, you are still appearing to them to be entirely too aggressive in going after what you want. Or, in the case of the opposition, they may see you as only slightly impatient and occasionally rude or brash in behavior. To truly be free, you have to remove the obstacle of too much desire resulting in aggression, or compromise in the case of the opposition by toning down your brash behavior and learning the virtues of patience.

WALKING IN ANOTHER'S SHOES

SUN

In relationships, the Sun serves to highlight the skills or qualities of the other person, and to warm and ignite their inner fire so that their true self can become alive for others to see and enjoy. Therefore, if someone has a planet squaring your Sun, there is something that you need to do so that your inner light can shine its brightest. The Moon of another person squaring your Sun indicates that you may have some emotional inhibitions or emotional scars that you need to deal with, and the only way to do that is to see the Moon person's point of view.

The opposition means that you need to reach out to the other person and change your behavior in a way that will indicate that you understand his side of things. For instance, Neptune opposing your Sun means that you may need to be more intuitive in your dealings with this person. With Uranus, you may need to understand their point of view in respect to trying new things, and by doing so, you may learn to love the excitement and unpredictability that comes with dealing with that person. Letting some of their Uranian excitement into your life will allow you to express your inner talents in a newer, more refreshing way.

MOON

Emotional issues are usually the problem when someone has a planet squaring or opposing your Moon. Perhaps you are overacting to that person, and in the case of Mercury, you may be communicating in a hysterical way. Try to see things from their side, and learn to control your emotional outbursts. Or maybe their planet is Mars, in which case they may see you as being indecisive or lazy. By walking in their shoes, you can see how you need to adjust your behavior to improve the relationship.

With the opposition, the emotional issues are not quite as

serious, so only a minor adjustment is required. The Moon relates to the past as well as to emotions, so you may need to let go of something in the past that happened between the two of you if, for instance, Pluto is the opposing planet, or you may have to become a little more realistic about the past if Neptune is the other planet.

MERCURY

Planets squaring your Mercury are an indication that you need to change how you talk to the other person, for there are communication problems. More importantly, you need to change how you think about the relationship, for how you think affects how you act, and therefore how the relationship proceeds. "We are what we think" is a very common phrase, and carrying that one step further, our relationships are what we think they are. The other person may see you as very undisciplined in your thinking if Saturn is involved, or he may see you as being too glib, or maybe scatterbrained if his Sun is involved. Figure out what he is thinking and adjust your behavior accordingly.

Of course, with the opposition, you need to do the same soul searching to see what he is feeling, only the problem is not as severe as that with the square, so you just need to try to meet him halfway where communication is concerned. Maybe you just need to explain things in a way that he can understand, i.e. speak in a more traditional way if his Saturn is involved, or maybe you need to ask his opinion more often rather than just sharing your thoughts and ideas if his Jupiter is the opposing planet.

VENUS

Where Venus is involved, squares and oppositions are not usually as big a problem as with some of the other planets, as

WALKING IN ANOTHER'S SHOES

Venus is overall a very loving energy, so even negatively aspected, it is still beneficial. Problems arise if we become too mushy or sentimental, or at the other end of the spectrum, if we are unable to express our feelings of love. With the square, the problem has reached the point where we must make a change. If Saturn is the planet involved, for instance, it may be that you are not showing the other person that you care about them because you perceive them to be negative and cold. Or the opposite may be true; you may be showing too much affection if they are more reserved in their emotional expression.

In the opposition, the issues are not as pronounced. For example, Venus opposite someone's Jupiter indicates that you need to tone down your amorous feelings. Opposite Uranus, you may need to allow the other person a little more freedom rather than smothering them, and opposite Pluto, you may need to show love by helping the necessary transformative process take place.

MARS

How does one walk in the other person's shoes if their Mars is being squared? First of all, understand that the other person may see what you think of as energy and enthusiasm as rude, crude or aggressive behavior. Next time, before you decide to do something that affects the two of you, ask the other person's opinion if Mercury is involved; if the squaring planet is Venus, eliminate brash behavior by trying to become more sociable.

For the opposition, you just need to pull back a little of your Martian energy, based upon the opposing planet. Saturn, for instance, may mean that the other person doesn't want to move as fast as you do, so you need to slow things down a bit. With Neptune as the opposing planet, you may need to try to understand a little better their vision of the relationship rather than going off on your own to implement your idea of what the relationship is.

Astrology & Difficult Relationships: WHY ARE YOU IN MY LIFE?

JUPITER

Expansiveness is Jupiter's modus operandi, and sometimes the other person doesn't want to expand. With a square, you might say that you are just too much of whatever it is they are bringing to the relationship. So if your Jupiter squares their Mercury, they may perceive you as being too general or impractical. If their Pluto squares your Jupiter, they may perceive you as dogmatic or sanctimonious, always fighting against their desire for change.

In the opposition, again we are dealing with exaggerated behavior, but on a smaller scale, and thus easier to fix. Jupiter opposing their Moon may mean that they are seeing you as a little insincere, perhaps self-indulgent, or full of grandiose ideas.

SATURN

A planet squaring your Saturn indicates that the other person sees you as pouring rain on their parade, no matter what the planet. With Mercury, you keep them from saying what they want to say, with the Sun, you keep them from expressing their true selves, with Pluto, you restrict their personal power. The obstacle you have to remove is the idea of limiting or restricting their activities. You have to somehow show them that the purpose of your Saturn is to bring discipline and focus for eventual success.

With the less difficult aspect, the opposition, your Saturn energy still limits or restricts them but in a lesser degree, and so the remedy is easier. Try to understand how they feel and then adjust your behavior accordingly. If your Saturn opposes their Jupiter, for instance, understand that to them you extinguish their optimism and ideas. As the Saturn person, you cannot become as jovial as the Jupiterian, but you can become less dour, and only a small effort is required here to improve the relating process.

URANUS

If your Uranus squares a planet in the other person's chart, they perceive you as an unwelcome agent of change. Or, they may see you as eccentric and out of touch with reality. Anyone with new ideas will eventually run into someone so against their ideas that it is like hitting a block wall. The square represents just that; this person is your block wall. So you have to find a way around, under, or over it. You cannot walk through it, and if you try to knock it down, you risk destroying the relationship in the process. So if the planet being squared is Saturn, you have to make your ideas seem practical, with Mercury, you have to make them appear versatile, interesting and fun, and with Pluto, you have to make them appear intensely powerful and life changing.

With the opposition, the change required is not so great. You need to tone down your eccentric behavior a bit, or present your ideas in a more conventional way. So if Uranus opposes Venus, for instance, you need to adjust your way of showing affection, perhaps toning it down a bit, or being less eccentric in your expression. If it opposes Neptune, the other person may see you as a bit impatient, unpredictable or unstable, again requiring that you adjust your behavior slightly to make them feel comfortable.

NEPTUNE

Neptune is the intuitional, psychically sensitive planet, and if your Neptune squares someone's planet, they may think that you are unrealistic, deceptive, flighty or just not thinking or acting logically. While you may have a much better understanding of the situation due to the intuitional quality of Neptune, if the other person thinks you are not living in the real world, they will not take you seriously, which is the obstacle to be removed. If your Neptune squares their Sun, for instance, the perception of you as unreliable or deceptive they may not express themselves truthfully to you.

In the case of the opposition, the perceptions interfering with relating are less serious, and require minor adjustments to get the partnership moving forward. For instance, if someone's Mars opposes your Neptune, you need to adjust your behavior slightly so that the Mars individual is not annoyed by what he perceives as inefficiency, confusion or daydreaming on your part.

PLUTO

Squares and oppositions to one's Pluto almost always deal with power and control issues, or the perception by the other person that there are power and control issues interfering with proper relating. If your Pluto squares someone's Moon, you are perceived as trying to control how they react emotionally, or that you are trying to dominate them or take advantage of them. It if squares their Jupiter, they may feel that you are trying to coerce them to do something unethical.

Oppositions are not as difficult to fix, yet the same issues are evident. The general perception of being controlled, coerced, or dominated by you needs to remedied by a moderate change in your behavior towards the other person.

CHIRON

If your Chiron squares or opposes a planet in someone's chart, they perceive you as causing hurt or pain in their life, depending up which planet is involved. If Chiron is squaring their Mars, the pain you bring relates to their greatest desires, and probably their inability to achieve them. If Chiron squares their Venus, the pain you bring may have to do with their love life or lack thereof. The obstacle to be removed is the idea that you bring only pain. What you want to do is be perceived as bringing healing and wise counsel. For instance, with a Mars person, you will have to focus on the positive and point out growth opportunities present to the partnership even though past desires or goals were not achieved (e.g., maybe they were the wrong desires, etc.). Also focus on the fact that lost love or past painful romance is a learning experience, preparing you for a better one in the future.

With the opposition, it will be easier to turn a painful situation into a healing one, again by focusing on the positive, growth elements of the situation, and showing the path forward.

JUNO

When your Juno squares or opposes a planet in another's chart, the other person may feel that you are not committed to the relationship. The feeling is stronger with the square than with the opposition. If, for instance, your Juno squares their Mars, the lack of commitment could be perceived as a lack of enthusiasm on your part in pursuit of the partnership goal. Actions speak louder than words, so with this person, you have to act in a way that will allow them to see that you are as committed as they are. With Mercury, the perceived lack of commitment may have to do with your less than stellar communication or your seeming disinterest in discussing partnership goals and plans. If you are committed to the partnership, say it in no uncertain terms.

With the opposition, the perception is not as critical, but nevertheless, the effort needs to be made to change it. You have to make the other person realize that you are truly committed to the partnership by adjusting your behavior. For instance, if your Juno opposes Pluto, change their perception of you as a domineering partner to one of a committed partner simply by letting them have more control in partnership decisions.

Astrology & Difficult Relationships: WHY ARE YOU IN MY LIFE?

CERES

This is the asteroid that brings in the harvest, i.e., brings things to fruition. If your Ceres squares a planet in someone's chart, from their perspective, you are standing in the way of their completing a project or achieving a goal. Therefore you need to assess your behavior to see what you are doing that is creating this obstacle. For instance, if the other planet involved is Jupiter, perhaps you are smothering their expansive efforts with too much mothering. If the other planet is Uranus, maybe you are suffocating their uniqueness by too much of the Ceres nurturing and therefore robbing them of their independence.

For oppositions, you need to reign in your Ceres desire to feed and nurture so that the other person can more fully utilize the energy of their planet. Ceres opposing Mars, for example, means that the other person feels that his energy is being drained, and your Ceres opposing Saturn would mean that the other person feels that you are interfering with their ability to stay focused and disciplined.

VESTA

Dedication and devotion are the keywords for Vesta, so a square to your Vesta indicates that the person has problems regarding your devotion or dedication. If your Vesta squares their Sun, they may feel that your devotion to the partnership is casting a shadow on their Sun, prohibiting their ability to "shine" or express themselves fully in the partnership. In this case, the obstacle is overcome by developing restraint. Devotion to a cause, a principle, a partnership is admirable, but if it overshadows the other person involved, it must be tempered.

The opposition requires less of an adjustment. Opposing Mars, for example, the person may feel that you are not exhibiting enough zeal in your dedication to the partnership goals, or, at the other end of the spectrum, they may feel that your excess devotion is draining their energy. With Saturn, they may feel that you are too lax and unfocused in your devotion, and with Mercury, they may feel you are not coming up with ideas for moving the partnership forward. Each case requires that you adjust your behavior so that you can become more in sync with the expectations of the other person.

PALLAS ATHENE

Any planet squaring or opposing Pallas Athene, the supreme strategist, is an indication that the partnership is having difficulties getting past the planning stage, the difficulties being more problematic with the square than with the opposition. If, for instance, Pluto is squaring Pallas Athene, the other person most likely perceives you as trying to shove your plans down their throat in order to usurp their authority. With Mercury as the squaring planet, there is a battle of minds to see who is the smartest.

The obstacle has to be overcome by defusing the battle mentality by reminding the other person that you are on the same side. You have to do this through humility rather than superiority, by admitting that you could be wrong, and by listening to other ideas and points of view that may be different from yours. With the opposition, the same remedies will work, although you don't need to make as large as adjustment.

Next, I want to deal with the signs, and the way I am going to do that is to present them by triplicity, i.e., mutable, fixed and cardinal, sometimes referred to as the crosses. We have much to learn by looking at the polar opposite of a sign, and the cross or triplicity within which the two signs fall.

Astrology & Difficult Relationships: WHY ARE YOU IN MY LIFE?

CARDINAL SIGNS

ARIES/LIBRA

If you have a planet in Aries opposing a planet in Libra in another's person's chart, the main area of contention is going to be related to action versus procrastination. At least, that is how it will appear to the other person. The Libra person will feel that the Aries person is moving too fast without thinking things through, and the Aries person will feel that the Libra person is wishy-washy and can never make up his mind.

Since we are dealing with the opposition, sometimes not that much of a move or adjustment is required by the parties involved to get the relationship moving. In whatever area of life the opposition occurs, if the Aries person will just slow down a bit, and if the Libra person will just accept that in dealing with this person, he will not be able to gather as much information as normal, then progress could be made. If your son is the slow-to-make-up-his-mind Libra person, and you are the pushy Aries father, know that he will take longer than you to make a decision, so prepare for it ahead of time. Rather than letting him frustrate you at a restaurant because he takes so long to order, call the restaurant ahead of time, find out what they serve and let your son know so that he can be thinking about it for a while. And if you are the son, don't tell your father that you are going to do something until after you have made up your mind, so that he won't rush your decision making process.

ARIES/CANCER

This is one of the squares found in the cardinal signs, and the friction is usually caused by the Aries brashness versus the Cancer sensitivity. Since both are cardinal signs, they are both

WALKING IN ANOTHER'S SHOES

capable of initiating action. It is the way in which they go about initiating this action that is the cause of their relationship issues. Aries is bold and will rush forth; the Cancer needs to go very slowly, testing the waters each step along the way. Cancers do not jump ahead like Aries. Cancers stay in their shell until they are sure that it is safe to come out. By that time, the Aries has long gone.

So how do these two relate? The obstacle that needs to be removed by the Aries person is brashness, and the only way to do this is to stop and think before speaking or acting. The Aries person must learn to censor his actions. The obstacle that needs to be removed by the Cancer person is excess sensitivity. The thin skin has to be toughened enough so that he can deal with the outside world without falling apart. If you are the Aries person and the Cancer person is your secretary, slow down before you walk up to her, take your time in giving instructions, instead of just bounding out of your office and yelling orders at her. As the Cancer secretary, know that you do not need to take everything personally. When your boss yells, he is not really yelling at you. He is just in a big hurry and doesn't have time to stop and smell the roses with you.

ARIES/CAPRICORN

This is a square between two natural born leaders, one very conservative and deliberate, and one very fast paced and active. The Aries person is full of new ideas and ready to put them into practice right away. The Capricorn person takes his time, follows the rules and does everything according to tradition. An uncle who frustrates you by telling "you everything in good time" when you are ready to do things now can be difficult to deal with. However, these two signs are not that different, and if you can appreciate the similarities, then the obstacle can be easier to overcome.

Astrology & Difficult Relationships: WHY ARE YOU IN MY LIFE?

One similarity is obvious; they are both cardinal signs and therefore both initiators of action rather than waiting for others to start things. Another similarity is that they are both natural leaders. We tend to think only of the fire signs as the natural leaders, but the sign of Capricorn is a leader as well. Think of its symbol, the goat, climbing to the mountaintop alone, going forward until it reaches the highest heights. Only a leader would do that.

So that frustrating uncle we talked about earlier has a similar goal, to be out in front. As the Aries person, you want to be out in front as well, to be first. But your Capricorn uncle wants to be out in front to get to the top. Knowing that the two of you have a similar goal, to be out in front, makes it easy to identify a way to eliminate the obstacle to relating. You as the Aries person can relate to your Capricorn uncle by slowing down a bit, for you know that you are both leaders in the end and you now understand that the reason he is slow and steady is that he wants to make sure he reaches the top successfully. Remember that even if you slow down, you are still out front, in the lead. Your uncle can easily learn to speed up a bit for the same reason once he understands that you are in a hurry to get going so that you can be in the lead. Working together, he can carefully guide the two of you to the mountaintop, and you can get both of you there with speed.

CANCER/LIBRA

Here we have the square between the sign of sensitivity and nurturing and the sign of harmony and beauty. You would think that these two would get along very well, but the emotional and mental perspectives are at odds and that is where the obstacle is created. The Cancer person can feel the other person's pain and that is how he is able to nurture others; he knows what they need because he can feel it in himself. The Libra person, on the other hand, doesn't sense what is in the other person, but he senses better than anyone else what is truly beautiful and harmonious, and knows instinctively how to achieve that beauty and harmony in someone else. And when it comes to achieving beauty, the Libra person does not necessarily take a soft approach. Remember that the symbol for Libra is the scales, which implies applying justice.

So the two signs are both looking for beauty in others, one by feeling and sensing the pain that is causing the ugliness in their life and lovingly helping the person to eliminate it. The other sign, Libra, looks for beauty in others, and by a tough kind of balancing of the scales, is able to achieve it. Bottom line: both have the goal of achieving beauty or balance. So if the bottom line is the same, the only problem relates to technique. Therefore, if you are the Cancer person, and your spouse is the Libra person, and the two of you are always at odds as to how to raise and discipline your children because you think he is too tough and he thinks you are too soft, you can stop arguing. The two of you have a similar goal, and you should be able to now understand why he is tough, and he should be able to understand why you can be soft and still achieve the same goal.

CANCER/CAPRICORN

This is the other opposition of the cardinal cross. This time, we are looking at difficulties to relating due to a focus on the home and the inner foundations versus an outwardly, worldly perspective. I have always felt that this particular opposition is one of the easier to deal with because the Cancer is sensitive enough to appreciate the solid qualities of the Capricorn and not be threatened, and the Capricorn is far-sighted enough to appreciate the firm foundation that the Cancer provides. If you are a Cancer and having problems relating to a Capricorn, or vice versa, then obviously you have not yet reached that level of appreciation.

The Capricorn says I want to go out into the world, and the Cancer says I want to stay at home. For the Cancer person to walk in the shoes of the Capricorn person, he would have to work on releasing his fear of the unfamiliar. To do this, he would have to learn to look at the world in a more impersonal way, and realize that everyone is not out to hurt him. The best way to do this is to change his perspective to include a little of how the Capricorn person sees the world. The Capricorn person, in turn, must walk in the Cancer's shoes by changing his totally impersonal perception of the world. He must add some feeling, some sentimentality, some nurturing. He must realize that there is a personal result of his ambitious actions. The phrase, "It's not personal, it's business," was more than likely first said by a Capricorn person. The phrase needs to be modified to, "It may be personal to someone."

LIBRA/CAPRICORN

Here we have harmony versus ambition. The Libran person wants everything to be beautiful and balanced, and the Capricorn person wants to win, to get to the top. Both, though, are concerned with fairness, justice and the law, so that is a good place to start in learning to understand the other person, and thereby learning how to overcome the obstacle that stands in the way of better relating.

Suppose you have a brother who represents the Capricorn point of view, and you represent the Libran energy. The two of you are always fighting over money, specifically how to handle your mother's estate. He wants to do things that you feel are totally selfish and in his own best interests. You feel that you want to do things that are in everyone's best interest. The situation has become so bad that you don't talk to him anymore.

To help you two relate in a better way, you need to appeal to his value system, to his innate desire for justice and fairness. As the Libra person, you detest arguing, but on the fairness issue, you probably will not argue because you are both on the same page.

WALKING IN ANOTHER'S SHOES

As a Capricorn, he will appreciate your references to law and tradition, and doing what's just. By finding common ground, you can begin the communication process again, and gradually find a way to deal with your differences that is fair to both of you.

FIXED SIGNS

TAURUS/SCORPIO

In dealing with the fixed signs, the word "fixed" is key in all of the situations. It means just what it implies, and so it is very easy to see the problems that the fixed signs have in relating to each other. No one will budge from his or her respective position. The Taurus/Scorpio opposition is related to passion and desire, but with Taurus, it is more material, and with Scorpio, it is more emotional. And they both will fight to the end, especially the Scorpio. So they should be able to make just a little adjustment to improve their relationship. If the Taurus person took into account the Scorpio's depth of feeling, and if the Scorpio could take into account the practical, down-to-earth side of Taurus, a meeting in the middle might be able to take place.

For instance, suppose you are the Scorpio and your daughter is the Taurus. You have never been able to get along with her; you always disagree on everything, and power struggles have surfaced constantly. You want one thing, she wants something else, you refuse to give in and she refuses to allow you to win. Right now, you are fighting over which university she should attend in the fall. If the two of you could find a way to step back from your anger and define a common goal, such as creating a list to identify why she is going to college or what she needs to look for in her college choice, or financial considerations. Then you both might be able to draw up a list of potential colleges that the two of you could agree upon. Then the two of you could contribute your respective talents, her strong will, and your steadfastness, and see the goal to fruition, that of choosing the most appropriate college that would fill her needs and at the same time, be agreeable to you. You need to learn to be a little less stubborn and more open to discussion and your daughter needs to learn to be a little less emotional and a little less controlling, and together the two of you can relate in a positive way.

TAURUS/LEO

One of the squares of the fixed cross, this can boil down to a battle of wills similar to the Taurus/Scorpio opposition. But since it is the square, the battle is more serious, and a bigger adjustment has to be made by the participants. Taurus and Leo are both fixed in their position, and the difference is that the Leo fixity occurs from a point in the center, from the self, and the Taurus is fixed on a point of desire outside the self. So the solution for the square is very easy to figure out. The Taurus person, when dealing with the Leo person, must turn his gaze inward, away from desires and towards his true self or center. The Leo person must do just the opposite; he must turn his gaze away from himself and look out.

Here is a practical example of what I am talking about. Suppose your Taurus Moon is squaring the Leo Sun of one of your co-workers. The two of you are in a power struggle over office procedures. You feel (and having a Moon in Taurus indicates that you feel very strongly) that your co-worker wants to take all of the credit and authority over an idea that you originated. You are very angry, but the first step towards creating a better relationship with this person is to remove the anger, for it is the main obstacle to proper relating. Walk in your co-worker's shoes by trying to see life from his perspective, a perspective that says that as a Leo Sun, he is naturally gifted administrator, and that he always sees things from a self-centered position. Realize this, and you will be able to rationally discuss the issues with the Leo person. On the other hand, if you are the Leo person, you probably don't understand all the fuss. Try seeing the situation from the perspective of a Taurus person who is wired to respond emotionally in a fixed and stubborn fashion whenever he feels threatened, and then you can realize that your behavior is making him feel threatened. Knowing this, you can adjust your behavior to be less threatening, which will entail looking outside yourself a little more. Then the two of you can work on a way to jointly present and implement the ideas that gives credit to the Taurus employee, and yet allows the Leo employee to skillfully administrate.

TAURUS/AQUARIUS

This is another of the fixed sign squares, and in this case, the two of you simply don't understand each other. The Taurus person is probably looking at the situation from the perspective of personal desires and personal pleasures, while the Aquarius person looks at the same situation from the standpoint of group desires and group pleasures. So the problem will be bridging the gap between the personal and the very impersonal.

The Aquarius person most likely seems cold to the Taurus person, and the Taurus person seems overly materialistic to the Aquarian. So if you are the Taurus person and you are dealing with a family member who is Aquarian in nature, rather than seeing him as cold and impersonal whenever he disagrees with you, try to understand that he is looking at things in a much broader, more general way. If you can learn to appreciate the fact that he brings to the relationship a broader perspective than yours, then you can go a long way in removing the obstacle to relating by letting him know that you value his advice. At the same time, he will see that he may have been wrong in thinking that you were only

Astrology & Difficult Relationships: WHY ARE YOU IN MY LIFE?

interested in personal comfort and desires, and will therefore be more receptive to your ideas. If you can learn to broaden your perspective by raising your desires from the strictly personal level to a more inclusive level, and if he can learn to take the coldness off his detachment by being more sensitive to you, then the two of you would be well on your way to positive relating.

LEO/SCORPIO

This is another of the fixed sign squares. The obstacle this time has to do with the Leo desire for individuality, and the Scorpio person's desire for control. The Scorpio person has a tendency to see life as a constant battle, and thus he is always strategizing, trying to figure out how to defeat the perceived enemy. The Leo person is interpreting everything from his self-centered position, and therefore his is not able to relate to the Scorpio person because he doesn't see past his center.

So, say for instance that you are the Leo employee and your new boss is the Scorpio person. The two of you cannot get along because you think he is trying to rein you in. You are used to making your own decisions and determining how to proceed on projects. You are great at giving orders and need no help in bringing a project to completion. Your new boss wants you to discuss everything with him first, and he has to approve every decision you make before you can implement it. You used to love your job, but now you are seriously considering looking for employment elsewhere.

For the relationship to work, you as the Leo must learn to view a world that includes others, rather than just yourself. From his perspective, your boss is offering valuable input; you may learn something from him. On the other hand, your Scorpio boss has to learn to lay down his desire to do battle for control, and by walking in your shoes, he will recognize that you are not an enemy, but a partner, and allow your input and creativity so that the two of you can create something greater than either of you could alone.

LEO/AQUARIUS

The Leo/Aquarius opposition deals with the struggle between the individual and the group. The Leo person needs to look outside himself, and the Aquarius person needs to develop his center before reaching out. Since this is an opposition, the adjustment required by both parties is small in order to meet in the middle. If someone's Leo Mercury is opposing someone's Aquarian Venus, for instance, the Leo person will have a difficult time communicating with the Aquarian person because the Leo person most likely will want to communicate only about himself (from the center) and the Venus person is only interested superficially because of his emotional detachment.

The Leo needs to pretend that he is the Aquarian person, and therefore try to look at how his words affect others around him, not only himself. The Aquarian person needs to learn to have a more personal touch with people, rather than just dealing with them superficially. Having a lot of friends is fine, but one only has true friends by digging deeper and allowing oneself to get to know that particular person very well. If the Leo looks out, and the Aquarian looks in, they will be able to talk to and understand each other.

SCORPIO/AQUARIUS

This fixed square deals with intensity versus impersonality. The Aquarius person is very superficial when it comes to relationships, and the Scorpio person is not superficial about anything. As a result, the two people just do not understand each other or their motives at all.

Simply put, the Scorpio person needs to get to the bottom of things, he feels deeply, he scrutinizes, researches, and agonizes over things. The Aquarian is impersonal in attitude, has many acquaintances but not that many really close friends. The goal of the Scorpio, which you would learn if you stepped into his shoes, is to develop inner resolve and willpower. The goal of the Aquarian is to learn true humanitarianism, the knowledge that we are all one, which again you would learn if you stepped into his shoes. Therefore, if the two of you are to ever relate, you as the Scorpio must realize that your Aquarian friend will give you a broader understanding of any subject the two of you broach together, and he, on the other hand, should appreciate the fact that you will give him a deeper understanding of the same subject. When you understand and appreciate the value of each other's contribution, then genuine relating can occur.

MUTABLE SIGNS

GEMINI/SAGITTARIUS

This is an easier opposition than some, because these are two signs that are fun on their own, and therefore when they meet in the middle, you have the possibility of a very enjoyable situation. The Gemini person loves to go all other the place gathering information or spreading information. The Sagittarius, on the other hand, is very one-pointed, since he already knows what he needs to know, or where to find the information, and stays right on track to find it or to lead others to it.

Therefore, the opposition arises because of the Sagittarius dogmatism versus the Gemini flexibility. All that is really required here is that the Sagittarian loosen up a little and listen to some other points of view, and the Gemini person needs to sit in one spot long enough to really understand the Sagittarian point of view well before moving on to another subject.

Therefore, if you are a father with Gemini Moon and it is opposing your son's Sagittarian Mercury and the two of you just cannot communicate, then you as the Gemini person need to stop flitting all over the place and listen to what you son has to say. Once your son realizes that you are actually listening to him and giving him a chance to explain his point of view, he will be more amiable to listening to your side of the argument, a view that is different from his perceived truth. The two of you may not agree initially, but at least you will be talking and that is the first step towards reaching a settlement that you can both live with.

GEMINI/VIRGO

A Gemini Sun person married to a Virgo Sun person may be considered disastrous by some for it represents one of the mutable squares. But what if the two people decided that they were going to make their marriage work by walking in the other person's shoes to overcome the issues to relating?

The difference between a Gemini and a Virgo is largely one of degree. They are both mental signs, since the traditional ruler of both is Mercury. They are also both mutable signs, meaning that they are both fairly adaptable, open to new experiences. But where they differ is in details. The Gemini person normally doesn't pay so much attention to them, while the Virgo person is obsessed with them. This is why the Gemini person stays in the mental realm, sometimes described as the ivory tower, while the Virgo, due to its earth element, is able to bring ideas from the mental level and actually manifest them. And it is by paying attention to the details that the Virgo is able to manifest things. The Gemini person feels that it is not necessary to spend so much time on the details since he won't be thinking about any particular detail for that long. His role is to gather lots of information but not necessarily to do anything tangible with it.

For these two to relate, the Virgo person must understand the airy, flexible nature of the Gemini and not expect that everything must be perfect for not everything has to manifest for the Gemini. The Gemini person, on the other hand, has to understand that once in a while he must slow down and work on one project long enough to see it come to fruition so that the Virgo partner will be fulfilled.

GEMINI/PISCES

Here we have a square based on feeling versus thinking. The Gemini person is, of course, the ultimate concrete thinker, while the Pisces could be termed the ultimate in feeling and sensitivity. These are two very different approaches to experiencing the world, and the problem for the relationship is that the two people don't always understand nor appreciate the importance of each other's approach.

Walking in the other person's shoes would require that the Gemini person admit that there is something to be said for simply knowing that something is right rather than having to prove it intellectually. The Pisces person, on the other hand, has to come down from the clouds occasionally and admit that the scientific, rational approach to reality can be just as valid, as is evidenced by all of the progress we as humans have made through research, study, and an intellectual approach to life.

So the next time that you are fighting with your mother-in-law, who seems to draw her information from the clouds, rather than being the rational, Gemini person who only deals in the facts, take a look at her intuitional conclusion and see if it does really make sense. Your mother-in-law needs to learn as well that taking a rational approach doesn't make her wrong; it just looks at the same facts in a different, more concrete way. She may realize that the two of you can come to the same conclusion, each in his or her own way.

VIRGO/SAGITTARIUS

Here we have a square with quite a large obstacle. The focus of these two signs is quite different, and seemingly unrelated. And yet, they must somehow be related for they are both on the mutable cross. Flexibility and a willingness to try new experiences are the trademarks of the four mutable cross signs. Sagittarius shows this flexibility quite easily; the Virgoan person less easily. And yet it is there. The Sagittarian is very blunt and the Virgoan very refined and discriminating.

Someone squaring one of your planets from Virgo is going to be very critical of how you do things. To walk in the Virgo's shoes will require that you use your optimism, of which you have much, to allow Virgo's criticisms to bounce off of you. And from the Virgo side, you must learn that too much attention to detail can detract from your enjoyment of life; the Sagittarian has much to teach you about trust, faith, optimism and truth.

The truth is that both of you, though you see life very differently, are just expressing two aspects of a whole. The Virgo person represents the beauty of creation, and the Sagittarius represents absolute faith and trust in a beautiful and bountiful world. If you can each remember the perspective offered by the other, then you should be able to appreciate that both perspectives are needed, and therefore realize the you are not against each other, but only expressing different aspects of the same thing.

Astrology & Difficult Relationships: WHY ARE YOU IN MY LIFE?

VIRGO/PISCES

This is another of the mutable cross oppositions. As such, both participants need to make a minor adjustment and the energy flow will be greatly improved. Traditionally, Virgo is very precise and exacting; Pisces is easier going and willing to go with the flow. How, then, can Virgo be classified as a mutable sign, and more importantly, how can the two signs meet in the middle?

Virgo is open to new experiences, which explains why it is still a mutable sign. It will make sure that all of the details are taken care of as it goes from experience to experience. By learning to be more accepting and less critical, the Virgo person can make the jump from totally Virgoan to a little bit Piscean. At the other end of the spectrum, the Pisces person can learn to be just a tad more discriminating, that is, learning that you cannot say yes to everything, and that they cannot help everyone. They can learn from the Virgo to pick their fights.

Therefore, if you are a Virgo person and your son-in-law is the Piscean person, you may have trouble with his dreamy qualities, the fact that he has problems holding down a job, and you constantly question why your daughter chose to marry him. But if you look closer, you will see that he is very supportive and gives compassionate understanding to your daughter, which is probably why she chose him. He, on the other hand, rather than being offended by your constant criticisms, should realize that you are someone who is able to achieve results in the real world, and that he can learn from you how to take his dreams and make them realities if the two of you could only become friends.

SAGITTARIUS/PISCES

The final square in the mutable signs, their main obstacles would be the single-pointedness of the Sagittarius person versus the flowing intuition of the Pisces. Sagittarius is depicted with the arrow because he knows where to shoot it, and then can follow the arrow with unerring precision. The moral makeup of some Sagittarian types is so strong that they can sometimes feel that everyone else is wrong. Pisces, on the other hand, gives a more accepting attitude, a willingness to listen to and embrace the opinions of others. So one says, how can you be so easily swayed, and the other says, how can you believe that you are always right.

If you have a planet in Sagittarius squaring a planet in Pisces in another's chart, your challenge is to figure out how to soften that unyielding position you maintain, so that your Pisces friend can get his or her ideas across once in a while. The Pisces person, on the other hand, should learn to appreciate your steadfastness and understand that you could help her learn how to accomplish more of her dreams through unyielding focus.

The next time your Sagittarian boss tells you to stop daydreaming and focus, realize that he is sharing with you his tool for success, that of single-pointedness. And the next time that you share one of your intuitional ideas with your Sagittarian boss, he should realize that you are sharing more than a dream, that you are giving him something worth considering as his next cause to steadfastly pursue.

The most important thing to remember about all of this is that squares and oppositions are really opportunities for us to learn how the other person thinks or feels. If we remember this whenever we are comparing our chart to another's, we will not see it as a bad thing but rather as a learning situation. The people who "square" us or "oppose" us are performing an important function in our lives. They are forcing us to deal with problem areas in our personalities and when we correct them, we are able to relate better to others.

CHAPTER EIGHT

WHEN SHOULD WE TAKE ACTION?

The answer to the question, "When is the best time to take action to heal a relationship?" is very simply, when the stars are working with us. In astrology, determining when to act and when not to act is a function of timing, and timing is determined by transits and progressions. Timing is everything, and knowing when to act to achieve the best possible result requires a thorough study of the transits and progressions relating to the issue at hand. In personal relationships, problems may seem insurmountable, but as astrologers, we know that there are times when seemingly insurmountable problems can be attacked successfully because of the outside help from the cosmos. So if you are in a difficult relationship and don't know if it can ever be fixed, look at the transits and progressions in the two charts and see if you can identify opportune times to try to mend the situation. Usually you can find something. If you cannot, it may be that the relationship is not meant to be a permanent one, and you need to start thinking about what that means. But if you feel that the relationship is fixable, then take a look at the timing issues.

So what kinds of things do you look for when you want to know the best time to try to fix a broken relationship? First of all, you need to identify the planets, signs and houses that would be most beneficial for fixing an ailing relationship. Relationships are ruled by Venus, Libra is the sign of relationships, and the seventh house is their domain in a chart. So the first thing to do is to look for opportune transits coming up involving the Venus of either person or for planets currently in the sign of Libra. Also, check to see the status of the seventh house of both parties. By status, I mean, what planets are currently transiting the seventh house, and also what natal planets in the seventh house may have transiting aspects from other planets coming up.

Secondly, the asteroid Juno has to do with committed partnerships, so you should make the same examination of Juno's situation in both charts, i.e., any upcoming transits or progressions involving Juno, the relationship of Juno to transiting Venus or to the sign of Libra.

The next areas you want to look at are the planets, signs and houses that are related to the issue that is causing the trouble in the relationship. For instance, if you are always fighting with someone over money, then you want to look at the money planets, signs and houses when figuring out the most opportune time to act to mend the relationship. If, for instance, you were fighting with your spouse over your children, the fifth house, Leo and the Sun would figure in, so you would need to check their current status.

Finally, you need to look at the planets, signs, and houses that rule the problem area in both charts. So, if the Sun rules your second house, and money is an issue, then you should take a look at what transits are coming up for your Sun, natal and progressed, into account also. For instance, if you see that transiting Saturn is going to be conjuncting your progressed Sun in a few months, you should start thinking now about how that is going to affect the way you handle or use money, and how that may help you to improve the relationship.

Now that you know the planets, signs and houses that you are going to be researching, the next thing to do is to identify those planets besides Venus and Juno that will be beneficial in relationship issues. Jupiter and Neptune both bring in compassionate, loving and expansive energies to whatever area of your life they touch, so if they are involved in a relationship area, so much the better. Jupiter will allow you to expand the good things about the relationship, and Neptune will allow you to visualize the perfect relationship and to dissolve anything that is getting in the way of manifesting the ideal.

Transits and progressions of the other two outer planets, Uranus and Pluto, will be wonderful times to update, change or transform the relationship. If you notice that one of these planets is going to be transiting a planet in your chart that is causing problems in a relationship, then you can be especially excited because you are being given the opportunity to use the energies of the planets to help you mend the situation. For instance, suppose you are in a difficult relationship and Mercury is one of the planets that conjuncts the other person's chart. You notice that Pluto will be squaring your Mercury in about two months. You can expect that during that time, you will be able to use the energy of Pluto to help get rid of a lot of the issues that are causing communication problems. All you have to do is be open to the idea of change.

Returns are also good times to proceed, for you will have a double dose of that particular energy. Returns usher in a new cycle, so no matter what has happened in the past, you have the opportunity to start fresh. The inner planets move so quickly that you have solar, lunar, Mercury, Mars and Venus returns ever year or two. And the outer planets take so long that you will probably only see a Uranus return, and that is if you live to be 84. But Jupiter and Saturn are just the right length of time to be of use to many people. Jupiter returns to its natal position every twelve years, and Saturn every twenty-nine and a half years. With Jupiter returns, you have the opportunity to open up a whole new dialogue and to start fresh in a positive and loving way. With Saturn returns, you will have the opportunity to make some better choices so that the course of the relationship will change.

Besides transits, progressions and returns, you should also be on the lookout for eclipses. Eclipses speed things up in the

WHEN SHOULD WE TAKE ACTION?

area in which they occur in your chart, or they intensify the effect of planetary energy if they happen to conjunct that planet in your chart that is creating the relationship difficulties. Therefore, if you know that an eclipse is coming up in your seventh house or in the sign of Libra, or that an eclipse is going to conjunct Venus, be ready to see some positive change in the nature of the relationship.

Finally, think about in advance how to best use the energies of the planets and signs in upcoming transits, progressions, returns, and eclipses, rather than just waiting for something to happen to you. In the final analysis, you are the creator of your life, so rather than believing that the planets "do things" to you, learn to figure out what you want to do in your life, and then use the energies of the planets and signs to help you to achieve that.

CHAPTER NINE

HOW TO ANALYZE YOUR DIFFICULT RELATIONSHIPS

Now that you have learned the hows and whys of difficult relationships, it is time to take a look at your own difficult relationships and begin the process of categorizing them so that you can understand and fix them. We will go through the process step by step, applying all of the concepts discussed in the previous chapters.

STEP ONE: The first thing you want to do is to compare your natal chart with the natal chart of the person with whom you are having problems. List all of the conjunctions, and determine the closest one. If there is only one conjunction, then this step is very easy, but if there are several conjunctions, you will have to study them carefully to see which is the closest. By closest, I mean the conjunction that is the most exact, that is, the conjunction that has the smallest number of degrees and minutes between the two planets. If there are no conjunctions, then by our definition, this is not truly a difficult relationship. Later on, we will look at the squares and oppositions that, as you know, can cause relationship problems because of obstacles and needed compromises. These, though, are more easily overcome than conjunctions.

HOW TO ANALYZE YOUR DIFFICULT RELATIONSHIPS

STEP TWO: Once you have identified the closest conjunction, you can then name the relationship based on the categories listed in Chapter Three. For instance, if the closest conjunction involves your Moon and the other person's Sun, the relationship, from your point of view, is one of Releasing the Past. From the other person's point of view, it is a Self-Awareness relationship. In this analysis, though, we are concerned only about answering the question, "Why are you in my life?", and so the process we are going through now will categorize the relationship from your perspective only, so the name of the relationship is Releasing the Past.

STEP THREE: Next, you will want to review the description of the conjunction in Chapter Two. In our example, you would want to re-read the section on the Moon. Then, do your own meditating and soul searching to determine what behavior you need to change in order to fix the relationship.

STEP FOUR: Next, you need to determine the best place to start to mend the relationship. We discussed in Chapter Six how trines and sextiles can be helpful in locating the areas of agreement which you can use as the springboard into other areas in the relationship that need improvement. Therefore, an analysis of the trines and sextiles in the relationship can give you the starting place.

STEP FIVE: Analyze the squares, oppositions and inconjuncts to get a better understanding of where the wide fissures exist in the relationship. Try to see life from their point of view in those areas. Review Chapter Seven if you need help.

STEP SIX: Finally, devise an action plan that you can follow. The action plan should address (1) the most immediate and pressing change that you will make regarding the conjunction,

Astrology & Difficult Relationships: WHY ARE YOU IN MY LIFE?

(2) the most immediate and best use of the trines and sextiles, and (3) the most immediate and pressing step you can take to remove an obstacle or imbalance in the relationship.

Here is an example. You determine that your difficult relationship with your sister-in-law is mainly a Mirroring relationship involving your Suns, so it is all about self-expression. Your strongest trine is between her Mercury and your Venus. Your closest square is between her Mars and your Saturn. The way this relationship has played out is that she is constantly borrowing your clothes and never returning them. She likes to go out with her girl friends and always leaves her children with you at the last minute. She is totally irresponsible as far as you are concerned. The only reason you put up with her is because she is your brother's wife and you love your brother very much. You are starting to sense that your brother is feeling caught in the middle, and you want to do something to improve your relationship with your sister-in-law for his sake.

You do some analyzing and soul-searching regarding the nature of the relationship, and now believe that because it is a mirroring relationship, there is something similar in your approach to life, and more importantly, there is something that you are learning from or mirroring to each other. You realize that you and your sister-in-law represent two extremes of the same Sun sign. You represent the serious and responsible aspect, and she is the irresponsible, fun loving side. In this set-up, she is mirroring to you how too much emphasis on fun can have its repercussions, and you are mirroring to her how too much responsibility creates an overly severe outlook on life. The key, you realize, is to learn from each other about how to balance your lives. Deep down, you wish that you could be more fun loving like her; you believe that deep down, she also wants to project a more responsible image. So, you develop the following action plan:

HOW TO ANALYZE YOUR DIFFICULT RELATIONSHIPS

(1) Using the Mercury/Venus trine as your starting point, you decide that you will take advantage of the fact that she loves to talk and that you love beauty and that the two of you together love to talk about and enjoy beautiful things. You decide to invite her to lunch, and to an afternoon of shopping.

(2) During this luncheon, you will attempt to be more fun loving than you normally are. You will not bring up issues regarding responsibility such as how she spends her money, or her house cleaning abilities.

(3) In line with the Saturn/Mars square, you will try to put yourself in her shoes. She sees you as the Saturn person who is always throwing water on her plans. You will make it a point to agree to do something with her that is totally her idea.

Keep your action plan simple. If you try to do too much at one time, you will almost always fail, and then you may give up. One small change can accomplish wonders, for the other person will make note, and then he or she will make one small change, and then things will grow exponentially, until you have a large change, and the relationship is healed.

Also, don't expect everything to happen overnight. It may take several overtures on your part to illicit a response from the other person. Many years of arguing and distrust cannot be eliminated in one afternoon. Be patient. Also, it may help to revisit the previous chapter on timing to learn when to expect some noticeable progress in the relationship. Just keep at it and eventually something should happen.

If however, you have waited a reasonable amount of time and have not seen any improvement, then you might want to take a look at your action plan and see if you need to make some adjustments. Perhaps you haven't done enough walking in their shoes; maybe you need to try a little harder to overcome obstacles presented by a square. Or, maybe you are not using the energy of the trine to its fullest potential. All master plans usually require

Astrology & Difficult Relationships: WHY ARE YOU IN MY LIFE?

some tweaking along the way. If you feel that you have honestly tweaked your plan to the best it can be, then you just need to be patient and allow it to do its work.

WHAT IF YOU DON'T HAVE THE OTHER PERSON'S CHART

This is a difficult problem, but not an impossible one. You can many times intuit the astrology of the relationship simply by looking at the issues and areas where you have problems, and the areas where you usually agree. If someone is always aggressively standing in the way of your doing what you want to do, or always arguing with you, then you know that somehow their Mars is probably involved. If someone is constantly creating upheaval in your life, then their Uranus is probably the culprit. If someone is constantly evoking old emotional responses from you, then more than likely your Moon is involved. If you feel that you cannot be yourself around that person, then they probably have a planet conjuncting your Sun. If you are forever trying to control someone's life and they won't allow it, then your Pluto may be the reason. If you are required to take care of someone else or are in someway indebted to or responsible for them, then Saturn is more than likely the planet involved.

You should be starting to see that it is not that difficult to dissect a relationship even without both charts. Sit down and honestly ask yourself what it is about the other person that makes it difficult for you to relate to them. You should also be able to identify areas where the two of you have agreement, the common ground, represented by the trines and sextiles. With this information, and with your own chart in hand, you should be able to come up with enough information to work on fixing the relationship.

HOW TO ANALYZE YOUR DIFFICULT RELATIONSHIPS

WHAT IF THE OTHER PERSON SIMPLY WON'T RELATE

We discussed this issue somewhat in Chapter Five, where we talked about how being overly rational or overly self-involved could create obstacles in a relationship. You may want to reread that chapter. If after doing that, you still don't know how to handle the issue, then you may need to forget about expecting the other person to work with you and accept that you will have to work alone at mending the relationship. Make the adjustments that are required from your side, and hopefully the other person will respond.

Sometimes, though, you can follow all of the outlined steps, and still come up empty where the relationship is concerned. You can look at the issues of timing, you can attempt to make contact at the most opportune moments and still fail. If this happens, if you have done all you can do, and you still cannot get the relationship going, consider that maybe the purpose of the relationship is to teach you detachment. By dealing with someone who refuses to relate, you are learning certain lessons about power and control and about learning to let go. Perhaps you are learning that you cannot control everything in your life, and that in this instance, you simply have to walk away.

IF YOU KEEP HAVING THE SAME TYPES OF RELATIONSHIPS

You probably have had a friend or know of someone who has had numerous failed romantic relationships with a certain type of individual and yet keeps attracting the same kind of person. Your friend wonders why his relationships never work out, and yet to you, the answer is obvious. For some people, though, things are not so obvious. It is always much easier to diagnose a relationship from the outside rather than when you are actually involved in it. Being in the thick of things removes perspective, so you cannot always see what you are doing wrong, or recognize any kind of pattern. Sometimes having patterns pointed out to us will allow us to fix the situation. But other times, it will only aggravate the situation if we are not yet ready to hear the truth.

There can be any number of reasons why we do not want to or cannot accept the truth. We may be emotionally "blind", or we may be too young emotionally to make the leap to a higher level. If you keep having the same kinds of relationships, then you need to take a look at your chart and note the status of your seventh house, the placement of the ruling planet and the aspects made to it, and the planets located in that house and aspects made to them. If, for instance, Neptune is involved, you may not be seeing things clearly and may need to ask for assistance from trusted friends. If Pluto is the ruling planet, you may need to totally transform your views of relationships and the types of people you with whom you should be relating. If Venus is involved, you may have to review how you show love to others since, after all, we attract to ourselves what we send out into the world. Trying to break old patterns can be difficult and you may have to spend some time figuring out the "why" before you can figure out the "what" to do.

POISONOUS RELATIONSHIPS

By poisonous relationships, I am referring to those relationships that are detrimental to both parties. Pluto is the planet that is usually associated with poisonous relationships. They are usually controlling relationships that have gone to extremes. But Pluto is not always involved. Sometimes these relationships involve people who are emotionally dependent upon one another, for instance the alcoholic and the enabler, or the abusive husband and the wife with low self-esteem, and often Neptune is involved.

The normal reaction is that these relationships should just be ended immediately for the good of both parties. Sometimes, though, the parties just cannot break the ties that connect them. In those cases, there may be a karmic tie, therefore many times Saturn, or the South Node, or the Moon is involved and the relationship has to be completed to learn the life lesson.

The difficult relationships that are being addressed in this book are not poisonous relationships. They are, for the most part, relationships that can be healed, and that can provide spiritual growth for both parties involved. A difficult relationship that has no hope of spiritual growth may be poisonous and should be ended. If you are not sure whether yours is a poisonous relationship or not, then you should examine the two charts together and see if you can discover a reason for the relationship to continue by categorizing it based on the categories in Chapter Three. A thorough analysis of the related charts can give indications of whether there is a spiritual tie or whether it should be ended. If there is a lot of violence, or aggression, or the Plutonian type of excessive control and power struggles, then maybe you need to classify the relationship as poisonous and simply get out.

NOT ALL RELATIONSHIPS ARE MEANT TO LAST FOREVER

This is a fact that we sometimes forget. We relate with others because there is a purpose. The purpose is usually mutual soul growth. If the purpose of the relationship changes, or if it has been fulfilled, then the relationship may no longer be necessary, and so it may end, or it may change or modify its quality to be more representative of the new purpose.

If a relationship is no longer necessary, that is, if it no longer serves a purpose, then it is supposed to end. If that is the case, then the lessons have been learned, or the debt paid. The person is now ready to move on and have new experiences with new people who will further the soul growth of one or both parties.

When a troubled relationship ends abruptly without a

satisfactory conclusion, the parties may be left feeling that they failed in some way. This is not necessarily true. If the necessary lesson has not been learned, there will be others who will come into the life to continue with the teaching. But more often, the lesson has been learned and the parties just have not realized it yet.

So how do you know when a difficult relationship is truly over, or if it is one that should continue? Astrologically, you can do several things. First of all, you can look at the transits that were occurring at the time the relationship ended. If any of the outer planets were involved, Uranus, Neptune or Pluto, then more than likely the relationship is definitely over. Uranus, Neptune and Pluto always clear the way for something newer, better, or more appropriate to soul growth. It may be that the difficult relationship ended because there was absolutely no way that the necessary lesson was going to be learned, and it was simply a waste of energy.

Finally, if the Descendant or planets in the seventh house are negatively impacted, it probably means that the relationship was destined to end. This is especially true if transiting Saturn was at the Descendant or was traveling through the seventh house, as this is sometimes indicative of a permanent ending for karmic reasons, and the same can be said of the Vertex transiting the seventh house, which brings a destined or fated quality to relationships.

So do not feel that you have failed if the relationship ends with things still up in the air. It may have ended because it was supposed to end. Sometimes you will find when relationships are ended by transits of Uranus, Neptune, Pluto, Saturn or the Vertex, there is another more exciting relationship waiting in the wings, and the things you learned from the old relationship will allow the new relationship to unfold. In other words, if the bad relationship did not end, the new one could not appear.

We have all heard many people say that we make all of our mistakes in our first marriage, or on our first child, so that the next one is better. Every major relationship we have changes us in some way, and if the change is positive, then we will move into our next relationship with greater understanding, strength and wisdom.

CHAPTER TEN

THERE IS NO SUCH THING AS A DIFFICULT RELATIONSHIP

In this final chapter, I'm going to ask you to do something that may sound a little strange. I want you to forget everything we talked about in the first nine chapters. That's because in this chapter, we are going to look at relationships from a totally different perspective, which means that none of the previous rules apply. In this chapter, we're going to start with the premise that there is no such thing as a difficult relationship and we are going to show how that premise is possible. It requires that you simply make a few changes in your basic approach to relationships and relating.

1. SHIFT YOUR EMPHASIS FROM YOUR PERSONALITY TO YOUR HIGHER SELF OR SOUL. Difficult relationships exist because our focus is on personality issues. Everything we talked about in chapters one through nine had to do with the problems of the personality. By that I mean that we looked at difficult relationships from the perspective of how they affected us **personally**. But suppose we could find a way to by-pass the personality and go directly to our higher self. If we deal with relationships from that level, then all of the personality issues will disappear, for at the soul level, they are irrelevant.

THERE IS NO SUCH THING AS A DIFFICULT RELATIONSHIP

Astrologically speaking, in order to work from the higher, soul level, you must always try to respond to the higher-level meanings of the signs, planets, and houses. Astrology is, after all, the study of how energies play out on various levels. For instance, the planet Mercury, on the physical level, often manifests as someone who has a lot of nervous energy and is constantly fidgeting. On the emotional level, it can create someone who goes back and forth on emotional issues and cannot make a commitment. At the mental level, it can create a highly intelligent and articulate person. But from the level of the soul, it creates someone who is able to create a bridge between the higher and lower because he can see both sides of any situation and intuitively knows how to combine the two for the best possible result. At the soul level, Mercury gives us illumination.

The ability to lift ourselves out of the personality realm and into the soul realm requires a certain amount of detachment. We discussed detachment a little bit in Chapter Five, and showed how someone can become so detached as to present an obstacle to relating. That is not the same kind of detachment we are talking about here. In Chapter Five, we were referring to a selfish, personality-centered detachment, where one looks at the benefits to oneself and if there are none, then the relationship is ended. Here, we are talking about spiritual detachment, which means that our personality or materialistic tendencies have been superceded by a more compassionate, encompassing love of humanity. Your personality issues are still there, it's just that they have taken a back seat to something higher. And when you allow your higher self to be in control, you allow that higher self to dictate how your lower self will respond. When the higher self is in control, the lower level personality issues are resolved in the best way possible.

2. ONLY DEAL WITH THE HIGHER SELF, OR SOUL, OF THE OTHER PERSON. If we can deal with ourselves at the soul level, then we can also deal with others at the soul level. And if we

deal with others at the soul level, then there cannot, by definition, be any personality differences. In other words, if you look for the soul, or the higher self, in the other person, and if you deal only with that, then there cannot be any difficult relationships because when we relate soul to soul, everything is perfection.

How do you recognize the soul in another person? An easy way is to only expect the best behavior from the other person, for his soul would do no less. The planet Jupiter definitely helps in this area, for it is the planet that gives us optimism and hope. If you are having trouble seeing the good in another person, look to the placement of Jupiter in your natal chart, and see if you are using those energies in the best possible way.

The ability to identify with others, to have compassion, and to forgive, are all qualities you need to possess if you want to recognize the soul in the other person. The planets Venus and Neptune can help in these areas, for they are both related to love and compassion. So if you think that you cannot love from a higher, impersonal level, which means showing compassion and forgiveness, then take a look at the position of your natal Venus and Neptune, and also look at the aspects they make to the other planets in your chart. Use those energies to call forth your higher self, and let those energies guide you in your relationships with others.

Every one of us has a spark of divinity. Yes, that includes the kid next door who broke your window, or the cranky grocery clerk, or the guy you got into a fight with at the bowling alley, even the criminal on death row. Every one has a spark of divinity; only sometimes it is buried so far under all the personality issues that we have a hard time finding it. But it is there, and you do possess the tools to find it. All it takes is a desire on your part to do so.

3. WE ARE NOT HERE ALONE. We do not incarnate alone. We incarnate in groups. But because we are so centered in our little self, the personality, we tend to miss the larger picture, the fact that we are here with others, our spiritual brothers, to do

THERE IS NO SUCH THING AS A DIFFICULT RELATIONSHIP

certain things together. So when we have relationship issues, rather than looking at the personality problems we are having with one particular individual, try to see the larger group and the larger group purpose and make your relationship contribute to that larger group purpose.

For instance, you may be feuding with your brother-in-law, and fail to see the larger picture from the perspective of the larger group, the family unit. All of the people in a family unit are there for a larger purpose; meditate on what you think that purpose is and see if you can relate to your brother-in-law in that way. Or, you may be fighting with someone at work, not taking into account that two of you are both working for the same company with the same goals.

If you can grasp the concept that we are not alone, that we are here to work with others, and that we can accomplish much more with others than we could by ourselves, then you will be able to simply forget about the problems of the personality. The little self just doesn't seem to be so important when you are looking at it from the higher perspective of group purpose.

4. LOOK TO THE COMPOSITE CHART TO SEE WHAT THE RELATIONSHIP CAN BE. We study composite charts of relationships because they show the dynamics of any given relationship. But the composite chart not only represents what the relationship is, but what it can be. It shows the relating parties the possibilities of the relationship if they can find a way to work out all of the kinks. Compromise is built into the composite chart, for it is the midpoint between the planets in each individual chart, and the midpoint is always where we meet in compromise. So if your Sun is at zero degrees of Gemini, and the other person in the relationship has the Sun at zero degrees of Libra, the composite chart of the relationship will have the Sun at zero degrees of Leo.

The relationship, then, will have a chance to show the Leo traits of generosity, warmth, and loyalty that each person could

Astrology & Difficult Relationships: WHY ARE YOU IN MY LIFE?

not do alone. The composite Sun at zero degrees of Leo is the meeting point, the result of the compromising and relating process.

An astrological chart can be read on many levels. Two people can have exactly the same chart, and yet be totally different. Much of the difference has to do with the level of advancement of the person with the chart. The same can be said of relationships. If the composite chart represents the relationship, then the relationship can be manifested on many levels, and the perfect manifestation of that relationship is the manifestation at the highest level.

You can use the composite chart of a difficult relationship to help you see what the relationship can be in its highest manifestation. So if you would like to know how what adjustments you need to make in a difficult relationship, look at the composite chart for the relationship and see what it tells you. Identify the planets in your chart that are causing problems in the relationship and see where those planets are located and how they are aspected in the composite chart. This will tell you how those planetary energies should be used to create the best possible relationship.

5. WE CAN CHOOSE HOW WE WILL REACT. Finally, we all have free will, and so we can choose how we will react in any given situation. We may not have any control over the actions of others, but we have total control over our own reactions to difficult situations. We can choose to react from the level of the personality, or from the level of the soul. The reactions are usually quite different, thus the outcomes will also be quite different.

Libra, the sign of decision and choice, has a lot to do with the kinds of decisions we are faced with, the kinds of choices we are required to make, and our latent abilities regarding decision-making. To analyze your life in terms of what to expect regarding major decisions and decision-making, look at the planets that are placed in the house that Libra rules in your chart.

But more important than your ability to make a decision is

THERE IS NO SUCH THING AS A DIFFICULT RELATIONSHIP

your basic life philosophy, which will have much to say about how you view the actions of others and therefore, how you will react to their actions. You can react in a loving yet detached way, or you can become overly emotional, or even physical in your reactions. Your basic life philosophy has a lot to do with ninth house issues, with the planet Jupiter and with the sign of Sagittarius, but it also has to do with the connection between your first house, fifth house and ninth house. These three houses deal with you, your talents, and your life philosophy.

Reactions also have a lot to do with the natal Moon, for the Moon relates to emotional responses. If your Moon is still controlling you, then you may have difficulty in choosing the proper way to react to others. If you find that your responses to others are usually overly emotional, then you need to take a look at how you are using those energies and try to find a better way to reflect the qualities of your natal Moon.

Choosing how you will react is probably the most important and yet the most difficult thing to change, for you can see how your reactions are based upon the personality which you have created in this lifetime. It requires that you do a total make-over of your personality. But if you can change the way you react to situations, you will change the nature of your relationships for the better. If your reaction is always one of calm understanding, compassion, and love, you will never perceive yourself to be in a difficult relationship.

These five rules for relating may be quite easy or very difficult, depending a lot upon your stage of spiritual development. But no matter where you fall on the spiritual scale, you can attempt all of them to some degree. Your ability to react as a soul can be enhanced if you truly want it to be, and the way to do that is to analyze your basic horoscope and then learn to use the energies in a positive way.

Every sign and every planet can aid in this process in some

Astrology & Difficult Relationships: WHY ARE YOU IN MY LIFE?

way, so I want to take a look at all the signs and planets in relation to their consciousness raising qualities. I will go through the signs first, and so you should pay particular attention to your Sun sign, your Ascendant sign, and any sign that is strong in your chart, for example, a sign which rules an angular house, or a sign in which you have a stellium of planets.

ARIES

Aries energy likes to start new things, to take the lead, so in your dealings with others, you will be the first one to try a new way of relating. Aries gives you the initiative to institute necessary changes without fear. Thus, you can use your Aries energy to help you initiate changes in how you react to others, and how you perceive yourself in relation to others, thus beginning the process of relating from the soul level.

TAURUS

People with Taurus strong in their charts usually have strong desires. These desires need to be lifted up so that they become aspirations. The difference between desire and aspiration is that the former relates to personality issues and the latter relates to the group or common good. You are well equipped to bring light into the world for you can see the highest ideal if you really try. And once you have seen it, you can apply this light to your relationships to lift to them their highest level. Taurean energy will allow you to put the goal of the relationship ahead of your own personal goals.

GEMINI

If you have a lot of Gemini energy in your chart, then you should be an excellent communicator. You bring people together,

THERE IS NO SUCH THING AS A DIFFICULT RELATIONSHIP

you spread the word, and you are great at seeing all sides of an issue. Therefore, you probably have very little problem relating. But if you do, call upon your ability to see the other person's point of view in order to lift any situation from the lower to the higher stage of relating. Talk through your differences and see the common links. The ability to see both sides gives you not only the ability to see the soul versus the personality in yourself and in others, but to see how they can be linked.

CANCER

You are the mother of the world, you sense what others are feeling and give them comfort, so you are one of the best ones to be able to shift the emphasis from yourself to others. Because yours is a sign of extreme sensitivity, you can sense, or intuit, the soul in the other person, and so can more easily address it than some of the other signs. You know how to hold a relationship together, and you use your famous Cancer claws to scoop up anything that is harmful to the relationship.

LEO

Despite what you may think, Leos can be very good at addressing the soul in others if they can learn to take the focus away from their little self and address their higher self first. That's the hard part. But any Leo who learns how to shift his focus from himself becomes a dynamo in the art of caring for and giving to others. The lion heart for which you are famous loves in a big way, and that is because when you approach others from the point of love, you are attracting their higher self. You are dealing with their soul.

Astrology & Difficult Relationships: WHY ARE YOU IN MY LIFE?

VIRGO

Virgos have a reputation, rightly or wrongly, of being extra critical. The soul is never critical, and so that is a way that you can tell if you are falling down into the lower self and need a lift. One way to help yourself stay out of the critical mode and into the higher, more accepting mode, is to emphasize one of your wonderful traits, that of service to others. Virgo types make the best doctors and nurses because they are at their very best when they are taking care of and meeting the needs of others. Do this and you will have no problem focusing on your higher self and the higher self of others.

LIBRA

Being one of the air signs, and adding to that the Libran ability to bring harmony and balance, makes this energy very conducive to dealing on the higher levels in relationships. Yours is a mental focus, and also one of fairness, so in relationships, you seem to intuitively know how to make everything work out smoothly and in a way that benefits both parties. The mental focus helps with detachment, and the love of beauty and harmony helps to be able to see the other person in only the best and highest light.

SCORPIO

Since this is a water or emotional sign, you may sometimes have difficulties getting to that higher level because you get caught up in emotional reactions. Possessiveness, jealousy, and intense passions can keep you trapped in the lower, personality field. The lesson of detachment, of letting go of those strong emotions, must be learned if you are to successfully learn to relate to others from the soul level. If you are victorious in your fight to overcome strong emotional attachments, then you will be able to use that power to hold the relationship in the highest light and to deal with each other from the highest level of soul love.

SAGITTARIUS

Your high idealism and your ability to see the higher vision should make this a lot easier for you than some of the other signs. You should be able to quite easily divorce yourself from the mindset of centering everything on your personality and lifting it to your higher self because you are far-sighted enough to know that there are things out there more important that just you. In the same way, your high vision almost forces you to see the highest in others, or at least the highest that is possible for them to achieve. And when it comes to choice, you almost always make the right one, for you have such a high set of personal and spiritual values.

CAPRICORN

You above all the other signs have the most potential for being able to deal with yourself and others from the soul level. You are the ultimate achiever. You have excellent perspective, are a brilliant strategist, and so always make the correct decisions to reach your ultimate goal. You just have to make sure that your goal, the thing that you want to achieve, is a spiritual rather than a personal goal, and success is guaranteed.

AQUARIUS

The most humanitarian of the signs, you can easily make the jump from the personal self to the higher self because you can innately see the universe as a whole. You know that we are all one, and so the differences we use to divide us are really arbitrary and not based on spiritual truths. Aquarians always love being part of

Astrology & Difficult Relationships: WHY ARE YOU IN MY LIFE?

groups, so the question for you, then, is which group are you going to join? Will it be the group that focuses on the personality, the lower self and lower level values that divide, or the group that focuses on the higher values of the soul that unite?

PISCES

Finally, the most compassionate of all the signs, you see others as yourself, and their pain and suffering, happiness and joy, or lack thereof, is also yours. The love of your brother comes very easily to you, and since the ability to love is directly related to the ability to see the soul in others, you have a jump on others in that department. The harder problem you may face is the ability to see the soul in yourself. Sometimes Piscean energy is so overwhelming, that if the person cannot or does not choose to see the highest possible good, then confusion, deception and escapism result. If you are confused about yourself, you may not see the divinity in yourself. If you are having problems identifying with your higher self, try to separate reality from illusion.

Next, we will look at the planets, and again, focus on those planets that are powerful in your chart, for example, the rulers of your Sun sign or Ascendant, planets that are angular, or planets that rule angular houses.

SUN

In spiritual astrology, the Sun represents the personality and the Ascendant represents the soul. The energy of the Sun, which is so vital and dynamic, is to be used to carry out the purposes of the soul. Look in your chart and try to see what the relationship between your Sun and Ascendant means. For instance, if you have an Aries Sun and a Capricorn Ascendant, your Sun sign

THERE IS NO SUCH THING AS A DIFFICULT RELATIONSHIP

qualities are supposed to be used to help you achieve mastery of whatever it is you are trying to achieve as a Capricorn. The Aries Sun energy would allow you to be pioneering and courageous in pursuit of the higher goal that is represented by your soul purpose, the Ascendant. A Taurus Sun and a Libra Ascendant would put your traits of desire and aspiration at the use of your Libran Ascendant whose main goal is to achieve harmony and balance, to be a peacemaker, and to learn to make the correct choice, especially in relationships.

MOON

The Moon is noted for its connection to the past, to ingrained emotional responses, to our foundation and early life. Sometimes the Moon can be a great aid in achieving the goal of living and viewing others from the soul level. But sometimes our Moon sign can be our biggest enemy, for if we have adopted a negative trait from our Moon sign, it is so deeply ingrained in our psyche, that sometimes it takes an explosion to root it out. Since the Moon represents the past, what we want to take from it are only the best qualities of our Moon sign, and all of the negative traits can be left in the past where they belong. Then, the best of our past, along with the traits of our Sun, can be used to fulfill our soul's purpose, represented by our Ascendant.

The triangle between the Sun, Moon and Ascendant is the most important one in figuring out who we are and why we are here. Spend a lot of time looking at that triangle in your chart, including the aspects made to each of them and the relationship of the rulers of the signs in which they are placed. I guarantee you will learn a lot about yourself and your soul or higher purpose.

MERCURY

This is the planet of mind, of mental processes, and

communication. How you think, how you talk, how you put your words together to make sentences are all indicated by the state of your Mercury. In relation to the soul, Mercury is the link between the lower rational mind, and the higher, intuitive mind. The intuitive mind is linked to our soul or higher self, and so if you can somehow connect to the higher, abstract mind, you are basically connecting with your higher self or soul.

Analyze the placement of your natal Mercury, the aspects it makes to your Sun, Moon and Ascendant if any, and also the aspects it makes to the rulers of the Sun, Moon and Ascendant, for these will tell you if you have a budding connection, or if you have things to work on before you can make the connection. For instance, if Mercury is conjunct your Sun, you probably have a very good, active and dynamic mind, and should be able to bring the personality under some sort of rational control, opening up the possibility for soul control. If your Mercury trines the ruler of your Ascendant, so much the better, for that means that you have a very easy flow between your soul purpose and your mental faculties.

VENUS

Venus is the planet of love and harmony, and the love that Venus teaches is an impersonal love. Therefore, if Venus is strong in your chart, you already know how to love impersonally. The way that you love impersonally is to love intelligently. To love intelligently means that you don't love on the basis of physical characteristics, or emotional responses. You love from the soul level. To love impersonally is to eliminate all of the personality issues from the equation, and see the other person only as a soul. When you do that, it is quite easy to love everyone.

If Venus is not strong in your chart, or if it is afflicted, you may have to deal with some old pre-conceived notions about what love is, how we show love, and how we attract it. If Venus

THERE IS NO SUCH THING AS A DIFFICULT RELATIONSHIP

squares Neptune, for instance, you may have some delusions about love, and need to learn how to get your head out of the clouds and see the reality of the situation. We use the word love and assume we are all talking about the same thing, but in reality, we are not all on the same page. If Venus is well aspected in your chart, you may have a higher developed definition of love than others who are still struggling to discern its true meaning. If you want to learn to deal with yourself and others from the soul level, you need to look at how you define love, and you can start by looking at how Venus works in your chart.

MARS

This is the planet of passion and desire, especially those desires and passions of the personality, the little self. So if your focus is on your lower self, Mars will oblige by giving you the energy to pursue those things that the little you wants. But if you switch the focus of your passions and desires to a higher level, Mars will oblige also, and help you pursue those higher-level passions and desires by giving you the stamina and energy for those pursuits. If Mars is strong in your chart, this is a plus, then, especially if you have already done the work to begin to see your life from the level of your higher self. You can then use all of your fighting instincts, your warrior traditions, to truly commit yourself to raising the level of your relationships. Mars is especially helpful once you have made the choice to view all of your relationships from a higher level, for it gives you the stamina and dedication to carry it out.

If you have made the choice to let personality issues rule your relationships, Mars can cause some problems, especially if Mars is afflicted. Mars squaring Saturn, for instance, will cause all kinds of restrictions and blockages and keep you from getting what you want. But if you make the correct choice, the higher level choice, even an afflicted Mars can be used to good advantage.

Astrology & Difficult Relationships: WHY ARE YOU IN MY LIFE?

Again looking at Mars squaring Saturn, restrictions and blockages will be removed by learning control lower level passions.

JUPITER

Jupiter is the planet of opportunity, expansion, fortune and spirituality. A well-placed Jupiter will be tremendously helpful in transferring your focus from your lower to higher self. More importantly, because of the optimism and trust implied by a favorable Jupiter, it will be quite easy for someone to see the higher and better side of others. In fact, you will probably expect it. Jupiter gives you the ability to hope, to believe that good things are possible for the relationship and the optimism to pursue those good things, and to love inclusively.

SATURN

The energy of Saturn can be used to help you deal with yourself and others from the soul level by presenting you with opportunities to make correct choices. By making correct choices, we are dealing from the higher or soul level. If we choose to be responsible, honest and fair in our relationships, then we are making the correct, higher-level choice. If, of course, we make incorrect or inappropriate or selfish choices, we are dealing from the personality level, and that is when Saturn steps in to show us what we did wrong. We interpret this from the personality level as a punishment or a limiting of our actions, but it is really the universe's way of helping us to learn how to act as a soul.

URANUS

Uranus allows you to take a revolutionary and innovative approach to the area of your life that it governs. If you can use this energy and apply it towards relationships, you can revolutionize

THERE IS NO SUCH THING AS A DIFFICULT RELATIONSHIP

them. Depending on other things in your chart, the new and revolutionary may not be welcome, especially if you are a strong Saturn person, or have Capricorn or Taurus strong. In that case, Uranus will feel to you like it is breaking up things in a rather uncomfortable and unpredictable way. To really use Uranian energies well, you have to be open to change, and have developed a certain amount of detachment where control of your relationships is concerned. If you can be detached, then you can let Uranus do its work of overhauling your relationships and showing you how they should really be.

NEPTUNE

If Neptune is strong in your chart, then dealing from the soul level should be very easy for you, because Neptune shows you the ideal, and if you follow its lead, you will behave in the highest and most ideal way, the soul-based way. Neptune, like the sign it rules, Pisces, brings the energies of compassion and sacrifice, so you would gladly sacrifice for the sake of the relationship as a whole. You are able to sense and easily understand the other person's point of view, and this allows you to make decisions based on what is right and loving and good.

PLUTO

A strong Pluto gives you the will and intensity to do just about anything you want. You will usually always win because you fight to the death. So imagine what that intensity could do if you choose to fight to the death to improve a troublesome relationship. You could single-handedly completely transform a negative relationship into a positive one. The only thing stopping you would be a focus on the desires of the lower self rather than the higher, a focus on personality control rather than soul relating.

Astrology & Difficult Relationships: WHY ARE YOU IN MY LIFE?

CHIRON

Chiron, the healer, the energy that helps us address our wounds and then use that experience to help others, is a powerful tool in mending difficult relationships. Chiron, because of its relationship to Sagittarius, will guide us in the direction towards healing, and in relationships, this guidance will help us to do the wise thing to heal our relationship and also help us to then be a role model or teacher for others also suffering in the same way. This is a powerful energy that should be used to benefit a circle larger than your own.

CERES

The energy of Ceres has been closely tied to that of the Moon and Cancer, in that it has a nurturing and mothering aspect. I believe that Ceres implies more than that, though. Ceres is related to the harvest, to things coming to fruition. Seeds planted can be finally made to reach maturity. A strong Ceres means that if you plant the seeds of reconciliation in a relationship, you will be able to see them reach maturity. You can "harvest" the relationship, and then, in Ceres fashion, mother it and care for it so that it continues to thrive and grow.

JUNO

This is the energy of the committed partner, especially the marriage partner. A well-placed or powerful Juno will be excellent for committing your time and energy to making the relationship work. With commitment usually comes success, for the more you give to a relationship, the more you get out of it. If you use your Juno energy in this way, meaning that you allow yourself to totally buy into the idea of the relationship, then you will not be easily discouraged or walk out when things get a little tough. You know

THERE IS NO SUCH THING AS A DIFFICULT RELATIONSHIP

that you are in for the long haul, and so you try to find solutions to problems. You are willing to compromise, and you are unwilling to accept failure. That kind of commitment has to make the relationship work.

PALLAS ATHENE

This is the energy of the strategist, the one with the brilliant mind. So with that much intelligence, you should be able to devise a formidable strategy for turning a relationship around, and you should be able to carry out the strategy with military precision. You should have the ability to figure out the opponent's weaknesses and to use this knowledge to better the relationship for both of you. Of course, this great military strategizing ability must be used to fight the right and correct battle; otherwise you may win the battle but end up losing the spiritual war.

Now that you have assessed your chart and know what energies you have to work with, its time to begin addressing your difficult relationships and applying the energies in the appropriate ways so as to achieve success. Success is defined as being able to operate from the higher or soul level perspective in all dealings. Remember, not only are you operating from your higher self, but you are also looking for that higher self in the other person and are relating only to that. Here are some examples of what I mean. In each of these examples, two ways of relating are offered. The second scenario, Scenario B, always requires that you call upon the energies of love, compassion, empathy and hope offered by your Venus, Neptune and Jupiter in addition to using the higher level energies of Mercury to communicate is a way that is illumined rather than argumentative. It requires that you call upon your Sun sign to create light and warmth, and that you bring forward only those qualities of your Moon sign that are positive. It requires that you use your Mars to energize and vitalize the relationship in

Astrology & Difficult Relationships: WHY ARE YOU IN MY LIFE?

a way that is beneficial to both of you, not just to your personal desires. The energy from Pluto should be used to eliminate the obstacles to successful relating, and the energy from Uranus should be used to create a new, better way of relating.

EXAMPLE ONE:

Scenario A

You have a mother who constantly picks at you. Ever since you were a child, she has criticized you and others, and you have a difficult time being around her. As soon as you are old enough, you leave home, and talk to her only occasionally, usually on holidays.

Scenario B

You have a mother who constantly picks at you. Ever since you were a child, she has criticized you and others, and you have a difficult time being around her. You call upon the Neptune and Venus in your chart to aid you in understanding that she is so critical of others because she is unaccepting and critical of herself, and that her comments to you are simply because she does not love herself. You vow to give her the unconditional love she needs.

EXAMPLE TWO:

Scenario A

Your husband left you for another woman. Your five-year-old son loves his father and wants to spend more time with him. You feel that your ex-husband does not deserve to spend time with

THERE IS NO SUCH THING AS A DIFFICULT RELATIONSHIP

your son because of the way he treated you; he broke up your family. So you make it very difficult for him to find a time that will work for you to schedule visits with your son.

Scenario B

Your husband left you for another woman. Your five-year-old son loves his father and wants to spend more time with him. You know that even though your relationship with your husband ended, the relationship between father and son is very important and so you cooperate with your ex-husband to schedule times for him to visit with your son. You call upon your Saturn to assist you in doing the correct and responsible thing.

EXAMPLE THREE:

Scenario A

Your cousin borrowed five hundred dollars from you three years ago and has not made any attempts to pay you back. You asked him about it last Christmas, and he laughed and said that you had more than enough money so why should he pay you back. You have not spoken to him since, and have refused to attend any family gatherings if you know he will be present. This has put a strain on your relationship with your aunt and uncle, his parents. You are saddened by this turn of events because you really do like your cousin but are determined to hold out because you know you are in the right.

Scenario B

Your cousin borrowed five hundred dollars from you three years ago and has not made any attempts to pay you back. You realize that your cousin has lessons to learn about finances, and that by not repaying you, he is creating more karmic problems for himself. You like your cousin and want to continue the relationship with him, so you decide to call upon the compassion and forgiving powers of Neptune and Venus and decide to treat the loan as a gift.

EXAMPLE FOUR:

Scenario A

Your father deserted you and your mother when you were a baby. Twenty years later, he has approached you and wants to have a relationship.* You flatly refused to see him, and vow that you will never forgive him for what he did to you and your mother and that you will hate him until the day you die.

Scenario B

Your father deserted you and your mother when you were a baby. Twenty years later, he has approached you and wants a relationship. You realize that people change, and the person who deserted you and your mother twenty years ago may have grown into a more responsible person, and therefore deserves a second chance. Besides, you know that harboring hate and resentment only hurts you, not him. You agree to meet your father for lunch and see if a relationship can grow from there.

THERE IS NO SUCH THING AS A DIFFICULT RELATIONSHIP

EXAMPLE FIVE:

Scenario A

Your boss is always taking credit for your ideas. Since he is your boss, you are afraid to confront him about this, and so harbor much resentment and anger. Because you are not releasing this anger the proper way, it is spilling out in the form of aggression towards co-workers and those you perceive to be weaker than you.

Scenario B

Your boss is always taking credit for your ideas. Even though he is your boss, you realize that you must summon up the courage to speak to him. You hope that by telling him about your concerns, he will try to be more sensitive to your feelings, and to give you credit for ideas where due. You realize that he may not be aware of the problem. You also realize that even if he does not respond in the way you wish, bringing the issue to the surface and speaking about it is still the right thing to do, and that no matter what happens, you know that you did the right thing. You use the strength and willpower of your Pluto and the passion of your Mars to help you handle the situation without fear, and to direct your energy in the right direction.

EXAMPLE SIX:

Scenario A

Your daughter-in-law is raising your grandchildren in a way that is totally contrary to the way you feel they should be raised. You always make it a point to tell her every time you see her do

Astrology & Difficult Relationships: WHY ARE YOU IN MY LIFE?

something wrong. Lately, you have noticed that she does not bring the children to visit you as often as before. You confronted her with this fact and the two of you had a huge argument and have not spoken for several weeks.

Scenario B

Your daughter-in-law is raising your grandchildren in a way that is totally contrary to the way you feel they should be raised. You realize that she has qualities that you don't have, and that even though she is not raising the children in the way you would, she is raising them in a way that reflects her qualities and her views of life. You call upon Mercury to help you see all sides of the issues and to understand that although you do not always agree with her point of view, you understand that it is our differences that make life interesting, and you relish the differences. You also call upon Uranus to help you see that maybe you need to shatter some of your old, preconceived notions about raising children, and allow yourself to be open to other methods.

EXAMPLE SEVEN:

Scenario A

Your best friend of twenty years is marrying your ex-husband. Your ex-husband wants your children to attend the wedding but you are totally against the idea, and have told your children so. Your anger has created a rift in your relationship with your children, but you are steadfast in your position that you will not speak to them if they attend the wedding. You also do not consider the future bride to be your friend any more and harbor much anger and hatred against both your friend and ex-husband. You feel that they have both betrayed you.

THERE IS NO SUCH THING AS A DIFFICULT RELATIONSHIP

Scenario B

Your best friend of twenty years is marrying your ex-husband. You ex-husband wants your children to attend the wedding. You realize that though your relationship ended with your ex-husband, you do not harbor anger, for you understand the reason for the relationship and more importantly, the reason it ended. You realize that now both you and your ex-husband must move forward, changed hopefully for the better by your experience together. You are happy that your children are going to be part of their father's wedding, as you consider them one of the good things that came out of your marriage. And, while the dynamics of your relationship with you friend will certainly change due to the marriage, you realize that she also played an important role in your life for many years, and that hopefully the two of you also changed each other for the better.

EXAMPLE EIGHT:

Scenario A

Your mother never gives you a birthday present, although you always give her one. She has always been selfish and unconcerned with the feelings of others. You have a baby who is now a year old, and she has also forgotten his birthday. You are so angered by her lack of caring for others that you decide once and for all that you will never give her another gift.

Scenario B

Your mother never gives you a birthday present, although you always give her one. You understand that your mother has still to learn the lesson of looking outside herself. You understand that

Astrology & Difficult Relationships: WHY ARE YOU IN MY LIFE?

when you give something, if you expect anything in return, then it is not really a gift. Additionally, you know that she is your mother and deserves your unconditional love, so you continue to give her presents at every birthday, and hope that she enjoys them.

EXAMPLE NINE:

Scenario A

Your next-door neighbor is constantly "borrowing" things from you and never returning them. You have asked him several times about returning your possessions and he tells you that he has already returned them, or that he never borrowed them from you in the first place. You finally reach your breaking point, so you confront him, have a fight, and vow to never have anything to do with him again. You son and his son are best friends, and you know that your fight will affect their relationship, but you don't care because you feel that he is a jerk and you don't want him in your life.

Scenario B

Your next-door neighbor is constantly "borrowing" things from you and never returning them. You understand that coveting someone else's property is a form of uncontrolled desire and that your neighbor has yet to learn that lesson. You understand that your role in this relationship is to help your neighbor learn detachment, i.e. to lift his focus from the material to something higher. You don't mention the items, although you will not loan him anything else, and hope that he learns detachment from you. Your neighbor's son has approached you and told you that he's sorry that his father hasn't returned the borrowed items to you. You tell the son that his father will return the items when he is ready and not to worry about it.

THERE IS NO SUCH THING AS A DIFFICULT RELATIONSHIP

EXAMPLE TEN:

Scenario A

Your son was killed by a drunk driver. The drunk driver happens to be your sister. You determine that you will never forgive her because your son can never be replaced and your sister should have to suffer forever for what she did to you. Your sister plummets into a suicidal state and you feel that this is what she deserves.

Scenario B

Your son was killed by a drunk driver. The drunk driver happens to be your sister. You know that your sister is suffering as much as you, and that for your own soul growth, you must forgive her completely, for harboring hatred and anger will only destroy you. This you realize because of the compassionate and forgiving power of Neptune. By offering love and forgiveness to your sister, she is able to transform her grief into a loving act. The two of you develop an organization to aid survivors of deadly auto accidents as a tribute to your son and her nephew.

    I could go on and on, but I think you are starting to get the picture. We can choose whether we will be happy or sad, whether we will forgive or carry grudges, whether we will be open or close-minded, and whether we will love or hate. The choices we make will determine the nature of our relationships. If we always choose Scenario B, we will never have a difficult relationship, only loving and learning experiences shared with other people traveling along life's path with us.
    When you meet up with a fellow traveler, smile and say hello instead of being cold and suspicious. Embrace your fellow

Astrology & Difficult Relationships: WHY ARE YOU IN MY LIFE?

travelers and help shelter them from the cold of life, and that way both of you will benefit. Remember that we are all headed in the same direction, and that we will all arrive at the same final destination, even though some will arrive there before others. If you get there before someone else, wait patiently for them, and lend a helping hand if they need it. Don't be too proud to take the hand of those who arrive before you . We lift those behind us, and we allow ourselves to be aided by those in front of us. That is how life works, and that is how we all learn to relate.

SOURCES

Bailey, Alice, *Esoteric Astrology,* Lucis Publishing Company, New York, NY, 1951.

Lofthus, Myrna, *A Spiritual Approach to Astrology*, CRCS Publications, Sebastopol, CA, 1983.

Oken, Alan, *Soul-Centered Astrology,* The Crossing Press, Freedom, CA, 1996.

Sakoian, Frances and Acker, Louis, *The Astrology of Human Relationships*, Harper & Row, New York, 1976.

Sakoian, Frances, and Acker, Louis, *The Astrologer's Handbook,* Harper & Row, New York, 1973.

Astrology & Difficult Relationships:
WHY ARE YOU IN MY LIFE?

Order Form

Please Print:

Name_____

Address_____

City_____State_____

Zip_____

Phone (_____)_____

_____ copies of book @ $14.95 each $_____

Postage and handling @ $1.50 per book $_____

Total amount enclosed $_____

Make checks payable to TLH PUBLISHING COMPANY

Send to:
TLH PUBLISHING COMPANY
1845 Cambria Avenue
Landers, CA 92285